EASY ELECTRO
PROJECTS FOR
TOY TRAINS

David E. Greenwald

KALMBACH BOOKS

Printed in the United States of America

First printing 1997

For more information, visit our website at
http://www.kalmbach.com

Publisher's Cataloging in Publication
(Prepared by Quality Books Inc.)

Greenwald, David E.
    Easy electronics projects for toy trains / David E. Greenwald.
    p. cm.
    Inlcudes bibliographical references and index.
    ISBN 0-89778-401-4

    1. Railroads—Model—Electronic equipment. 2. Electronics—
Amateurs' manuals. I. Title.

TF197.G74 1997   625.1'9
                                                  QBI96-40799

Book design: Mark Watson
Cover design: Kristi Ludwig

Contents

Acknowledgments

I am indebted to many people whose assistance was critical in writing this book. Allan Miller and Dick Christianson greatly encouraged me in this endeavor. Will Huffman, Mark Kobernick, and Patrick Wotus read and offered useful comments on parts of the manuscript. Anne Wilson improved my computer skills and struggled with me to translate the computer files that became this book. Amir Karmin offered useful suggestions for improving my photography. Art Sposto introduced me to several circuits that appear in this book.

I owe a special debt to my wife, Heleen, and my son, Elie, for encouraging me and bearing with me throughout this project. Heleen read through the manuscript several times, greatly improving its readability. She and Elie assisted in the photography.

Introduction

This book draws on a generation of experience with electronics among model railroaders. Books meant for scale modelers by Don Fiehmann, Paul Mallery, and Peter Thorne are full of useful ideas and insights, and I have learned much from them. Nevertheless, circuits designed for scale railroading often are not suitable for tinplate use. Toy trains draw much heavier currents and operate mostly on AC. Even when they are converted to DC operation, a measure I recommend, complications arise and must be dealt with. As a result, circuits designed for scale operation usually must be modified for tinplate use.

The circuits in this book have been designed and constructed specifically for tinplate use. Every one has been built and tested, and some have been in service on my layout for years. My prime concerns are reliability and simplicity. Nothing kills interest more quickly than continuing struggles with balky switches, temperamental E-units and other nuisances. I believe that there is no reason for toy train operation to be an exercise in frustration, and I want to show ways in which electronics can reduce the aggravation factor considerably.

HOW TO USE THIS BOOK

Read this section and the following sections thoroughly, especially the discussions of soldering and safety. Each chapter is a more or less self-contained unit, describing one or more closely related projects. After you have decided to construct a project, read the chapter carefully, referring to the diagrams and photos when the text mentions them. The combination of text, diagrams, and photos provides a much clearer picture of what you will be doing than text alone can offer. Note that in the diagrams, electrical junctions are indicated by heavy black dots. If wires cross without a dot, they are not connected. If you feel uncertain about the basics of electricity, I recommend Peter Riddle's primer on tinplate wiring, *Greenberg's Wiring Your Lionel Layout, Vol. I: A Primer for Lionel Train Enthusiasts*, Greenberg Publishing Company (now Kalmbach Publishing Co.), 1991.

The discussion of each project, except the very simplest, is divided into the following sections:

• A description of the circuit and how it works.

• A list of parts, materials, and tools required for the project. This list may be somewhat long, but many of the same items appear over and over in different projects.

• A section on preparing the parts and mounting them. Where to put things and how to make sure they stay put are unglamorous but critical matters. I have tried to deal with these problems using the simplest, least frustrating techniques.

• A section on wiring the circuit. Once you know that everything is going to stay put, wiring becomes infinitely easier.

• A section on how to test and install the project, including alternative uses and strategies.

Look for definitions of italicized words in the glossary.

PARTS, MATERIALS, AND TOOLS: WHERE TO GET THEM

Learning something for the first time is a messy business. If that is what you are doing, you should take

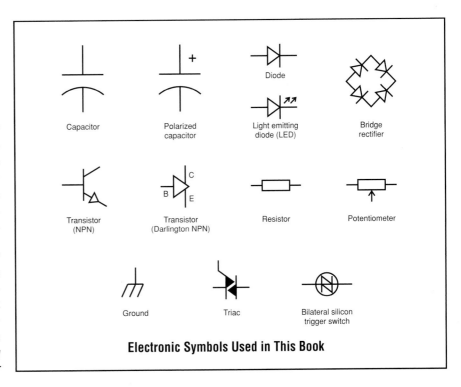

Electronic Symbols Used in This Book

it as given that you will have some burned-out circuits and ruined parts. Most electronic parts are not expensive. The biggest part of their cost consists of the time and energy spent getting them. Buying extra parts at the outset is cheap insurance against the inconvenience of replacing them.

For parts, materials, and tools, there are three main sources: Radio Shack, independent dealers, and mail-order houses.

Radio Shack, in thousands of locations worldwide, is the all-purpose chain store of electronics. With stores in just about every mall and shopping center, it is the ideal place for beginners. In many areas, in fact, Radio Shack is the only retail source of electronic parts, tools, and materials. Like a hamburger chain, Radio Shack has a uniform menu. Unlike a hamburger chain, Radio Shack can often special-order items that do not appear in the catalog. Wherever possible, projects in this book are designed to use Radio Shack parts, and Radio Shack catalog numbers are listed in parentheses. Many parts also have generic numbers, and these are noted in the text.

Independent electronics dealers represent a second source for parts and tools. They are not as common as Radio Shack stores, but if you have an independent dealer near you, you might want to look into it. Especially if the sales personnel are knowledgeable and helpful, it might be well worthwhile to patronize an independent dealer.

Mail-order houses are a third source for parts and tools, with decided advantages and disadvantages. They are indispensable if there is no retail dealer nearby, and valuable if an uncommon part or a large quantity of parts is called for. Mail-order houses usually have a more complete inventory than local retailers or Radio Shack, and their prices tend to be somewhat lower. However, they also charge shipping and handling fees ($5 seems a common figure) and sometimes require minimum orders. Some charge for catalogs as well. Many mail-order houses accept credit card orders by phone, and you can expect to receive your order in a few days.

A few required parts not stocked by Radio Shack are available from mail-order houses named in the text. Their addresses and phone numbers are listed in Appendix B. Other mail-order houses and independent dealers may also stock these parts. Additional parts and materials for projects can be found in hardware stores, stationery stores, discount houses, and even supermarkets.

HOW TO SOLDER

It is unfortunate that the thought of soldering intimidates so many people, for soldering is not difficult. It does not require expensive equipment or unusual skills. It consists only of following a simple procedure and using a little care. Furthermore, soldering is absolutely indispensable to electronics. In reliability and permanence, nothing surpasses a well-soldered joint. To solder, you will need the following equipment and materials:

Soldering pencil and soldering gun. For electronics, a low-wattage (15 to 30 watts) soldering pencil is best. More wattage means more heat, and too much heat destroys electronic parts. Radio Shack's 15-watt model (64-2051) works well with small parts. For heavier work, (e.g. soldering wire to track) a 50- to 100-watt soldering gun (64-2193) is necessary. I use a 100-watt gun. Usually soldering pencils come with small stands. Radio

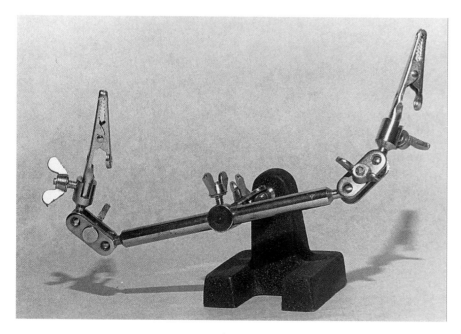

Helping Hands Project Holder

Shack also sells a separate stand (64-2078), with a sponge for cleaning.

Helping Hands. Helping Hands (64-2093) is a project holder that keeps things still while you work on them. It will spare you infinite grief.

Other items

• Wrench or screwdriver for loosening and tightening the nuts on the soldering gun. These nuts are usually 3/8". But check to make sure.

• A soldering heatsink (276-1567). This protects small parts from heat.

• Needle-nose pliers (64-1812 or 64-1844) For working on large parts with a heavy-duty soldering gun, I use a pair of needle-nose pliers as a heatsink, wrapping a rubber band around the handles to hold the pliers closed.

• A damp sponge for cleaning tips of soldering pencils and guns.

• Solder. Thin .032" rosin-core solder (64-005 or 64-009) meets most electronic requirements. Thicker solder is awkward to use, and acid-core solder corrodes the joints.

• A desoldering braid (64-2090). Occasionally, we need to undo our handiwork. A desoldering braid consists of a long strip of woven copper. To use it, place the braid on top of the joint, and heat it with a soldering pencil or gun so that braid sops up the solder by capillary action. As you use up one section of the braid, cut it off and go on to the next.

• Medium-grade sandpaper. For shining parts and removing oxide.

The procedure for soldering is as follows:

Before you plug in the soldering tool, loosen its tip and then tighten it. If you are using a soldering pencil, you can do this with a pair of pliers. If you are using a soldering gun, you will need a 3/8" wrench (or in some cases, a screwdriver) to loosen and then tighten the nuts securing the tip. This breaks up a layer of oxide that reduces the flow of heat. Since oxide can build up quickly during heavy use, you may have to repeat this procedure while you are soldering. Let the gun cool first.

Plug in the soldering tool. Make sure the cord isn't where it could get tangled and pull the hot tool down on you. Be certain that you have enough ventilation, as molten solder gives off lead fumes.

Clean the tip of the soldering tool by running it over the damp sponge.

Coat the tip of the soldering tool with solder. This is known as tinning it. Touch the solder to the tip, and the solder should flow instantly. If it doesn't, the tip isn't hot enough yet. Tin larger surfaces and thicker wires before joining them. Most electronic parts have leads that are pretinned, which makes the job easier. If you are working with fine, untinned copper wire, sand it until it is bright and shiny.

Make sure that the joint you are soldering is clean and strong mechanically.

Clamp the project in the Helping Hands (or something similar) so that it stays put.

If the joint is near a heat-sensitive device such as a transistor or diode, clamp the soldering heatsink onto the lead between the joint and the device. For small components, use Radio Shack's soldering heatsink. For larger components, use a pair of needle-nose pliers with a rubber band wrapped around the handles to keep them closed.

Holding the tip of the soldering tool against the joint, touch the solder to the joint (not the tip). The solder should flow like liquid silver through the joint. As soon as it does, remove the tip. If you work fast, you reduce the likelihood that heat will damage a part.

If you have never done this before, practice with some wire. As you will see, the actual process of soldering takes only about a second. Everything else is preparation.

SAFETY AND CARE OF PARTS

All the projects in this book use the low-voltage output of transformers or power packs. No project uses 115-volt AC house current. In general, safety is largely a matter of common sense. Soldering pencils and irons should be treated with respect, as they can remain hot for several minutes after they are unplugged. Cyanoacrylate (CA) adhesives such as Crazy Glue should be used with special care, since they can bond to skin in seconds. Finally, adequate ventilation is a must, since hot solder, silicone sealant, and many other substances give off irritating or hazardous fumes. On the whole, however, if you read labels and heed the warnings, you should have no problem.

You should also exercise care in handling parts. Many are sensitive to heat, and some to static. Keep static-sensitive parts in the conductive foam they come in until you are ready to install them. When you remove the foam, avoid touching the pins, and keep the parts, pins down, in an aluminum pie tin. It may be a good idea, especially on dry winter nights, to use a static-draining wrist strap (276-2397). Many parts are also sensitive to shock. If you drop them, they may suffer internal damage, even though they look unharmed.

1

Circuits with Light-Emitting Diodes (LEDs)

A SIMPLE LIGHT-EMITTING DIODE (LED) CIRCUIT

Light-emitting diodes have a multitude of uses in tinplate operation. They can light bumpers, bridges, and towers—in fact, just about anything requiring a small red, green, or amber light.

HOW THE CIRCUIT WORKS

Diodes are the simplest semiconductor devices, with two internal parts and two terminals. Light-emitting diodes (LEDs) are designed to generate light in a variety of colors when a small direct current (DC) is passed through them. LEDs are much closer to scale than most toy train bulbs, and they consume far less current; if LEDs are properly installed and

---

PARTS, MATERIALS, AND TOOLS

Parts

LED or LEDs (as many as needed in whatever colors desired): e.g. 276-021, 276-022, 276-041, 276-026. Do not use blinking LEDs for this circuit.

Resistors, one for each LED: 1 kilohm (1 K), .25 watt (271-1321)

Rectifier diode, IN4001 (276-1101) or IN4003 (276-1102) 1-amp unit

Materials

Wire (22 to 26 gauge)

.032 rosin-core solder (64-005).

Damp sponge

Medium-grade sandpaper:

1/16" or 3/32" heat-shrink tubing (278-1627)

Tools

15- to 25-watt soldering pencil (64-2051 or 64-2070)

Needle-nose pliers (64-1812 or 64-1844)

Wire stripper/cutter (64-1952 or 64-2129)

Helping Hands or similar project holder (64-2093)

Small (1¼") paper clip.

Hair dryer

Soldering heatsink (276-1567)

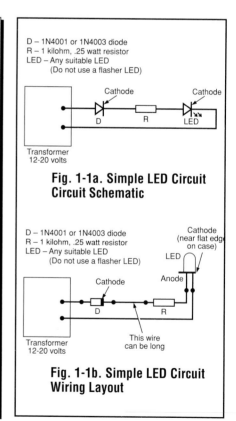

Fig. 1-1a. Simple LED Circuit Circuit Schematic

Fig. 1-1b. Simple LED Circuit Wiring Layout

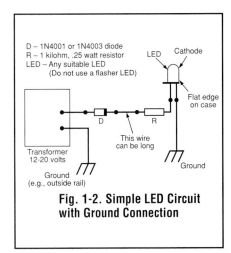

D – 1N4001 or 1N4003 diode
R – 1 kilohm, .25 watt resistor
LED – Any suitable LED
(Do not use a flasher LED)

LED   Cathode

Flat edge on case

D   R

This wire can be long

Transformer 12-20 volts

Ground
(e.g., outside rail)

Ground

Fig. 1-2. Simple LED Circuit with Ground Connection

used, they almost never burn out.

Unlike lightbulbs, however, LEDs require a little preparation and two extra components. But this additional circuitry is extremely simple. It is so simple, in fact, that building an LED circuit is a good way to begin toy train electronics.

LEDs run on DC. Tinplate transformers, however, provide AC. That AC must be *rectified*, or converted to DC. The easiest way to do this is to use a second type of diode, the *rectifier* or *power diode*. Rectifier diodes, like LEDs, come in a variety of sizes and shapes. They differ in the amount of current (*amperage* or *amperes*, commonly called *amps*) they can pass and the amount of electrical pressure (*voltage* or *volts*) they can withstand from a current flowing in the wrong direction. The latter is called *peak inverse voltage*, or PIV, for short. In general, the larger a diode, the more current it can carry.

The most useful rectifier diode for LED circuits is the 1-amp unit, with PIVs ranging from 50 to 1000. Two types, the 1N4001 (276-1101), with a PIV of 50, and the 1N4003 (276-1102), with a PIV of 200, are particularly useful for tinplaters. While there are some occasions when a diode with a PIV of 200 is necessary, most of the time the 1N4001 will do. For up to three

LEDs, the 1N914/4148 switching diode (276-1122) will also work.

A diode rectifies AC by permitting the current to flow only one way. Because AC changes its direction every 1/120 second, only every other pulse—half the current, in other words—gets through. Since a single diode passes only half the AC wave, it is called a *half-wave rectifier*. Usually, however, that is sufficient for powering LEDs.

An LED needs DC, but not too much—generally not more than about 20 milliamps (mA). Too much current will burn it out. Therefore, it is necessary to install a *resistor*, a device that limits the flow of current. Resistors are rated in *ohms* and *watts*. An ohm is a measure of a resistor's ability to restrict the flow of current. Restricting the flow of current, however, also releases heat, which the resistor must be able to dissipate if it is not to burn out. A watt is a measure of a resistor's ability to dissipate heat. Wattage is found by multiplying the amperage and the voltage. Generally, for LEDs in tinplate applications, a 1000-ohm

(1-kilohm or 1-K) resistor, rated at .25 watt, is suitable.

Unlike lightbulbs, LEDs and power diodes are *polarized*, Each has a positive pole (the *anode*) and a negative pole (the *cathode*), and each pole must be connected properly. In a typical LED circuit, this means that the cathode of the LED must be connected to the anode of the rectifier diode, or vice versa.

As shown in figs. 1-1a and 1-1b, all three devices—the LED, the rectifier diode, and the resistor—are connected *in series*, like beads in a necklace. In the circuit schematic, the arrow points to a line that indicates the cathode of a rectifier diode. That line corresponds to the band on the device, which makes it easy to avoid connecting a diode the wrong way. The cathode of an LED is indicated by a flat area or notch on the edge of the case, and its lead is shorter than that of the anode.

Figures 1-1a and 1-1b show the diode circuit with a return wire. But a separate wire is really unnecessary. Figure 1-2 shows how it is possible to use a ground

Fig. 1-3. LED Installed in Homemade Bumper

Fig. 1-4. LED with Its Wiring Exposed, Showing the Current-Limiting Resistor. Note the heat-shrink tubing on the right.

connection, such as an outside rail, as a return path for the electricity. In fig. 1-3 an LED is used to illuminate a homemade bumper; fig. 1-4 shows some of its wiring and its resistor.

CONSTRUCTION OF THE CIRCUIT

Construction of the circuit consists of joining the parts together. The resistor should be within 1" of the LED. The rectifier diode, how-

ever, can be near the power source. The circuit does not need to be mounted on a base. Construction steps are as follows:

❏ Straighten the small paper clip.

❏ Plug in the soldering pencil and let it heat up.

❏ Cut the leads of the 1-kilohm resistor to about ¾".

❏ Make two or three small closely spaced loops in the end of each lead: Wind the end of each lead around the straightened paper clip, and squeeze the loops tight and close together with the needle-nose pliers. The loops should be about ¼" from the resistor. It is much easier to use the paper clip as a form than it is to try to wind the resistor leads directly around the leads of the LEDs. See fig. 1-5.

❏ Clamp the LED in the Helping Hands. Notice that the anode is the longer lead. The cathode, besides being the shorter lead, is identified by a flat spot or notch on the side of the case.

❏ Slide a coiled end of resistor lead onto the anode lead of the LED until it is about ¼" from the case, and then squeeze it tight with the needle-nose pliers.

❏ Clamp the soldering heatsink onto the LED lead between this joint and the LED, as shown in fig. 1-6.

❏ Holding the tip of the hot soldering pencil against the joint, touch the solder to the joint (not to the tip of the soldering pencil). The solder should flow through the joint almost instantly.

❏ As soon as you see the solder flow through the joint, remove the soldering pencil. Trim any excess lead from the LED.

❏ Get a wire long enough to go from the resistor lead to your power supply, and strip ½" from each end.

❏ Solder this wire to the other resistor lead the same way you soldered the resistor to the LED.

❏ Near the power supply, use the same procedure to solder the lead from the cathode (banded end) of

Fig. 1-5. Using a Paper Clip to Coil a Wire or a Component Lead

the rectifier diode to the wire you worked on, on page 10. Don't forget the heatsink. Trim the excess lead.

❏ Now get a second wire long enough to go from the LED either to the other terminal of the power supply or to a ground connection, such as an outside rail. Strip ½" from the end of this wire, and slip a ¾" length of ¹⁄₁₆" or ³⁄₃₂" heat-shrink tubing onto it, about 2" from the end.

❏ Solder the second wire to the cathode lead of the LED. Trim any excess lead. Then slide the heat-shrink tubing over the soldered joint, all the way up to the case of the LED. The heat-shrink tubing should cover all the bare metal.

❏ Use a hair dryer to blow hot air on the heat-shrink tubing. It will shrink in place within a minute. This reduces the likelihood of a short circuit if the wires and leads should be squeezed together.

❏ Connect the rectifier diode to one terminal of the power supply. Use the fixed-voltage terminal of your transformer, if it has one.

❏ Connect the second wire to the second terminal of the power supply or to a ground. If you connect the second wire to a ground, make sure that the power supply has a ground connection also. On transformers with a fixed-voltage supply for accessories, one terminal is designated the ground connection and should be connected to the outside rail of the track. Locating the rectifier diode near the AC power supply has an additional advantage. It can power not just one LED, but an entire array. An eight-position barrier strip (274-670), as shown in fig. 1-7, and a jumper (274-650) make wiring this type of installation even easier. Make sure that each LED has its own 1-kilohm current-limiting resistor.

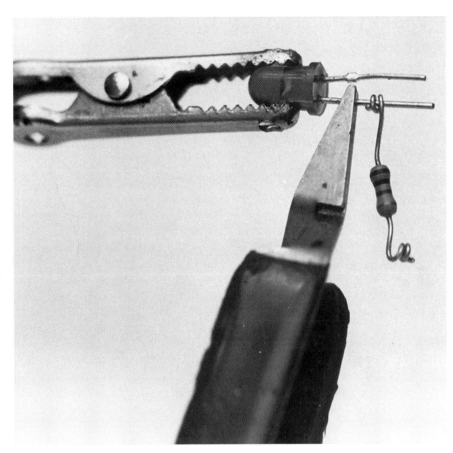

Fig. 1-6. An LED Ready to Be Soldered. Note the soldering heatsink between the joint and the LED.

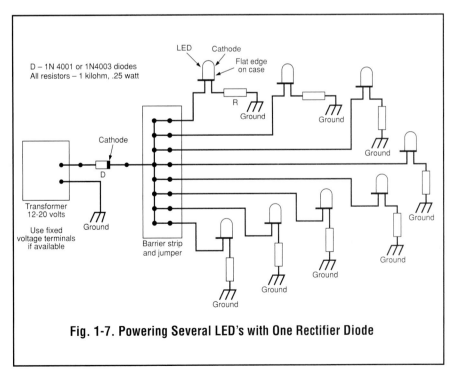

Fig. 1-7. Powering Several LED's with One Rectifier Diode

LED PANEL INDICATORS FOR 022 AND K-LINE SWITCHES

Lionel 022 switches and all K-Line remote-control switches are wired so that their controllers indicate which way the switches are set. Unfortunately, the controllers are obtrusive and do not easily lend themselves to control panels with track diagrams. It is possible to correct this situation with LEDs and SPDT switches or push buttons that fit nicely in a track diagram. LED circuitry replaces the red and green lightbulbs and, besides looking better, uses far less current.

HOW THE CIRCUIT WORKS

As figs. 1-8a and 1-9 show, this circuit corresponds closely to that of the original 022 controllers. The ground (center) binding post of the 022 switch goes to the center terminal of an SPDT switch, while the wires from the end binding posts go to the end terminals of the SPDT switch. LED circuitry replaces each lightbulb. Each LED, together with its resistor and rectifier diode, is connected between the center terminal of the SPDT switch and the end terminal that throws the switch in the direction opposite that indicated by the LED. Thus, an LED indicating that the switch is set straight is connected to the terminal that throws the switch curved. And an LED indicating that

the switch is set curved is connected to the terminal that throws the switch straight.

You can use push buttons instead of an SPDT switch. See fig. 1-8b. But the same considerations apply: each LED, together with its resistor and rectifier diode, is connected to the terminals of that push button that throws the switch in the direction opposite from that indicated by the LED.

The unusual wiring of this circuit results from the design of the 022 switch. (The 112 Super O switch is similar in design.) Each switch motor contains two hollow coils or solenoids that pull a steel plunger in either direction, throwing the switch. Each coil is connected to a set of contacts that open as soon as the switch is thrown. If, for example, the switch is thrown straight, the contacts connected to the coil that threw the switch in that direction are opened, and that coil is disconnected. At the same time, a second set of contacts, connected to the coil that throws the switch curved, is closed. Now current flows through the second (curved) coil. But the current does not throw the switch curved or overheat the coil, because of the green bulb in the controller. This bulb, which is connected in series with the curved coil, acts like a resistor, allowing enough current through the coil to light the bulb, but not enough to throw the switch or burn out the coil. Since the switch is already set straight, this bulb has to be green.

Moving the controller to throw the switch curved again shorts out, or bypasses, the green bulb. The coil now receives the full flow of current, which throws the switch. In turn, throwing the switch opens

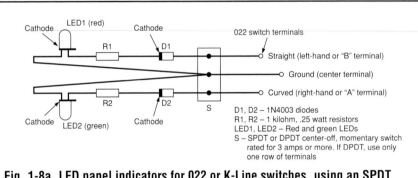

Fig. 1-8a. LED panel indicators for 022 or K-Line switches, using an SPDT switch or half of a DPDT switch

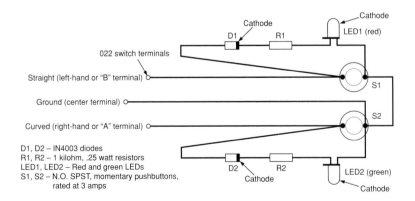

Fig. 1-8b. LED panel indicators for 022 or K-Line switches, using pushbuttons

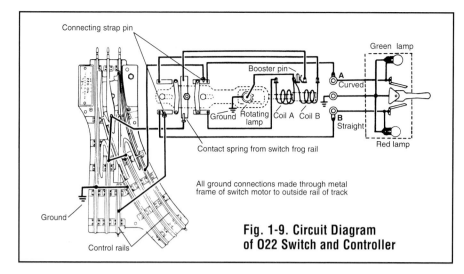

Fig. 1-9. Circuit Diagram of O22 Switch and Controller

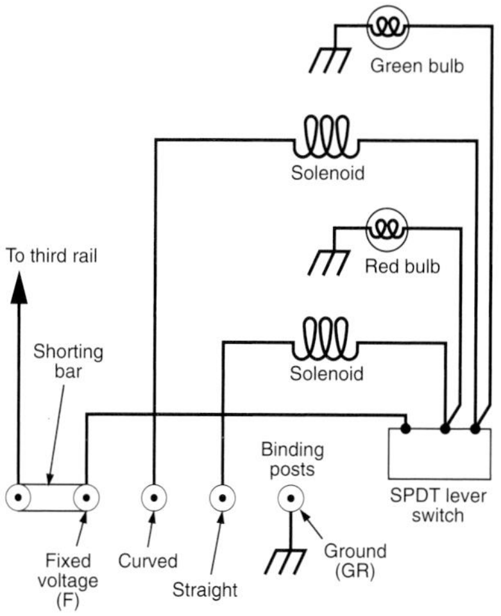

Labels in figure: Connecting strap pin; Booster pin; Green lamp; A Curved; Ground; Rotating lamp; Coil A; Coil B; B Straight; Red lamp; Contact spring from switch frog rail; All ground connections made through metal frame of switch motor to outside rail of track; Ground; Control rails

Labels in Fig. 1-10: Green bulb; Solenoid; Red bulb; Solenoid; To third rail; Shorting bar; Binding posts; SPDT lever switch; Fixed voltage (F); Curved; Straight; Ground (GR)

Fig. 1-10. Wiring of K-line Remote Control Switches

the contacts to this (curved) coil and closes the contacts to the other (straight) coil. Now current flows through the straight coil and the red bulb in the controller. Since the LEDs simply replace the light-bulbs, they must also be connected in series.

As fig. 1-10 shows, the wiring of K-Line switches is identical except for two items. In addition to the bulbs in the controller, K-Line switches have a pair of red and green indicator bulbs mounted on the switch itself. And instead of two sets of spring contacts, K-Line switches use an SPDT micro switch to shift power from one solenoid to the other.

CONSTRUCTING THE CIRCUIT

Constructing the circuit is a simple, two-stage procedure. Each LED is first soldered to its resistor and rectifier diode, forming a single assembly. Each assembly is then soldered to the proper switch terminals. See figs. 1-8a and 1-8b along with figs. 1-11 and 1-12.

Make sure that the rectifier diodes are lN4003, 200-PIV units (276-1102), because they are part of a circuit containing coils (in the switch motors). When the current flowing through a coil is suddenly turned off, a momentary high voltage appears. Known as *back electromotive force* (back emf for short), this voltage can destroy parts not designed to withstand it.

First, construct each LED assembly as follows:

❏ Clamp an LED upside down in the Helping Hands.

PARTS, MATERIALS, AND TOOLS
Parts (per switch)

Two T-1¾ LEDs, one red and one green (276-022 and 276-041). These colors match those of the bulbs in the original controllers. Other colors will do just as well.

Two snap-in holders for the LEDs (276-079). If you want to splurge, use chrome holders (276-080) instead.

Two 1-K, .25-watt resistors (271-1321)

Two lN4003 rectifier diodes (276-1102)

One SPDT (single pole, double throw) center off, momentary toggle switch with contacts rated at 3 amps or more (Hosfelt Electronics 51-219 or Mouser, l0TC245, either of which will fit in a ¼" hole). You can also use Radio Shack's larger DPDT (double pole, double throw), center off, momentary switch. (275-709), rated at 20 amps). If you choose a DPDT switch, you will be using only one row of three terminals. Whatever switch you choose, it must be a center off, momentary switch—that is, one that springs back to a center off position when released.

Another alternative is to use two N.O. (normally open) momentary push buttons, rated at 3 amps or more (e.g., 275-1556). See figs. 1-8b and 1-11.

Other parts, materials, and tools are the same as in the preceding circuit. If you use Radio Shack's 20-amp switch, you can solder the connections, which may require using a heavier (40- to 100-watt) soldering pencil or gun. Or you can crimp the wires onto female quick-disconnects (64-3058) and push the disconnects onto the switch terminals. A crimping tool (64-904), designed just for the purpose, makes this work easier.

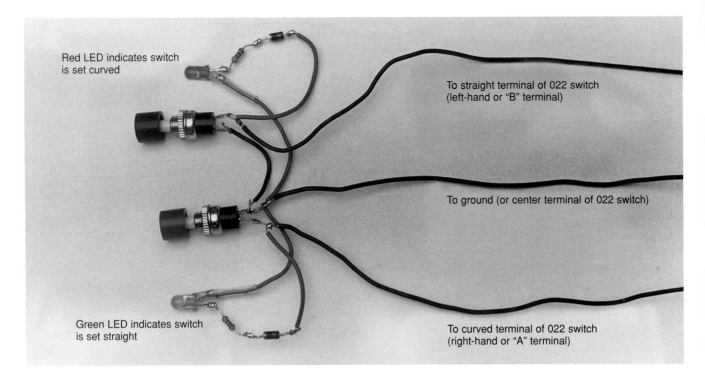

Red LED indicates switch is set curved

To straight terminal of 022 switch
(left-hand or "B" terminal)

To ground (or center terminal of 022 switch)

Green LED indicates switch is set straight

To curved terminal of 022 switch
(right-hand or "A" terminal)

Fig. 1-11. Panel Indicator Circuit for 022 Switches, Using Push Buttons

❏ Trim the leads of the 1-kilohm resistor down to 1", and coil the ends on the small paper clip that you straightened.

❏ Slide a coiled end onto the anode (the longer lead) of the LED, and squeeze it with the needle-nose pliers. Attach the soldering heatsink between the joint and the diode, and solder the joint.

❏ Trim the leads of the rectifier diode to about ½".

❏ Slip the remaining end of the resistor onto the cathode lead of the rectifier diode (that is, the lead connected to the banded end), squeeze it with the needle-nose pliers, attach the soldering heatsink, and solder it.

❏ Cut two pieces of wire, each about 2" long, and strip ½" from the ends. You can make these wires shorter or longer to fit the layout of your control panel.

❏ Coil one end of each wire, as you did the resistor leads.

❏ Solder one wire to the remaining (cathode) lead of the LED, and the other to the remaining (anode) lead of the rectifier diode.

❏ Slide a ¾" length of ¹⁄₁₆" or ³⁄₃₂" heat-shrink tubing over the first wire until it covers the solder joint with the cathode of the LED.

❏ Use a hair dryer to blow hot air on the heat-shrink tubing, shrinking it in place.

❏ Repeat the entire procedure with the other LED, resistor, and rectifier diode. Trim any excess leads or bare wire when you have finished.

The next task is to solder each assembly to the correct switch terminals—those throwing the switch in the direction opposite that indicated by the LED. To determine what goes where, first examine your 022 switch. See figs. 1-9 and 1-13. Hold the switch so that the three binding posts face you. The connection to the left-hand binding post, labeled "B" in figs. 1-9 and 1-13, throws the switch straight, while the connection to the right-hand post, labeled "A," throws the switch curved. The center post is a ground connection that energizes the switch when connected to either end post.

If you have a K-Line switch (fig. 1-10), hold it so that the row of five binding posts faces you. The binding post labeled "GR," which is adjacent to the switch motor housing, is the ground terminal. Next to it is the binding post that throws the switch straight. The next binding post throws the switch curved. The remaining two binding posts, joined by a metal bar, are power terminals, one for fixed voltage from the transformer, and one for power from the third rail. As is the case with the Lionel 022 switches, connecting the appropriate binding post to the ground energizes a solenoid, throwing the switch.

Next examine your SPDT (or DPDT) switch. See fig. 1-12. The handle should move in either direction, springing back to the center position when you let go. If it doesn't, either it is the wrong type of switch or it is broken.

14

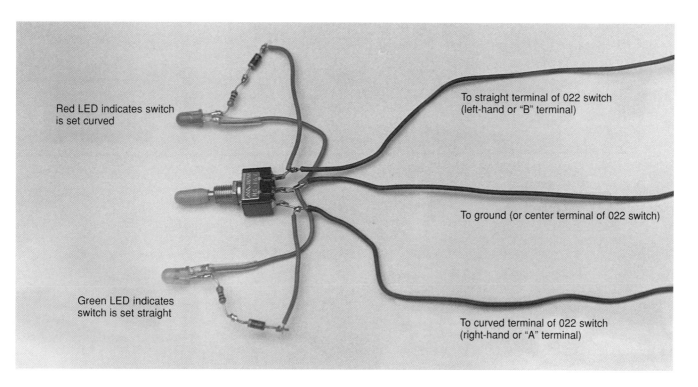

Red LED indicates switch is set curved

To straight terminal of 022 switch (left-hand or "B" terminal)

To ground (or center terminal of 022 switch)

Green LED indicates switch is set straight

To curved terminal of 022 switch (right-hand or "A" terminal)

Fig. 1-12. Completed Panel Indicator Circuit for 022 Switches, Using an SPDT Switch

This type of switch is usually constructed so that throwing it connects the center terminal to the terminal at the end opposite the way the switch handle points. To find out if that is true of your switch, perform the following test. Connect two wires to your transformer. Then connect one of those wires to the center terminal of the SPDT switch, threading it through the hole. Turn the power on, and throw the switch in each direction while you touch the other wire to each end terminal. A spark will indicate when the end terminal is connected to the center terminal.

Now you can attach the LED assemblies to the wires from the 022 switch. Owners of K-Line switches can also use this procedure, making appropriate changes for the different locations of the binding posts.

Attach the LED assemblies as follows:

❑ Using figs. 1-9 and 1-13 as references, label the wires from the two end binding posts (A and B) of the 022 switch.

❑ Strip about ½" from each end. The third wire, from the center terminal of the 022 switch, is a ground connection. Strip about ⅝" from one end of this wire. Incidentally, you don't have to connect the ground wire to the center terminal of the 022 switch, as long as you connect it to the ground somewhere else.

❑ Use the small paper clip to coil the ends of each of the 2" wires attached to the LED assemblies.

❑ Slide the coiled ends onto the stripped ends of the wires coming from the switch. Push the coiled ends almost up to the insulation. First, attach the wire from the cathode of each LED to the ground wire. Then attach the wire from the anode of each rectifier diode to the wire throwing the switch in the direction opposite that indicated by the LED. Thus, a green LED, indicating straight, is connected to the ground and to the wire from the A

or right-hand binding post of the 022 switch, while a red LED, indicating curved, is connected to the ground and to the wire from the B or left-hand binding post.

❑ Squeeze the coiled ends tight on the switch wires, and solder them.

Attach the three wires to the SPDT switch, as shown in fig. 1-12. The ground wire goes to the center terminal, while the wires from the end posts of the 022 switch go to the correct end terminals of the SPDT switch. Bend the end of each wire into the shape of a V. Then slide it through the hole on the switch terminal and squeeze it tight. But do not solder these connections yet.

If you are using push buttons, instead of an SPDT switch (see fig. 1-11), you must also attach a short wire, called a jumper, to the ground wire. The jumper must be long enough to go from one push button to the other. Coil one end of the jumper and solder it to the ground wire the same way you attached the LED assemblies to the other wires. Connect the ground wire to a terminal on one push button, and the jumper to a terminal on the other. Then connect each of the other two wires to the remaining terminal on the correct push button.

Before you solder the wires to the switch or push-button terminals, make sure that no adjacent wires, terminals, or component leads touch each other. Then test the circuit by throwing the SPDT switch each way or by pressing each push button.

Once the LEDs are installed, they should work just like the light-bulbs in the original controllers. If they don't, the LED or switch wires are probably crossed. You may be able to correct the problem by exchanging the connections at the A and B binding posts of the 022 switch. When everything is working properly, you can solder the remaining connections.

Finally, install the entire assembly in your control panel. Push each component through its hole from the back of the panel. Push the LEDs through without their plastic holders, so that they protrude from the front of the panel. Tighten the locknut on the SPDT switch. Then snap the LEDs into their plastic holders and press them into their holes.

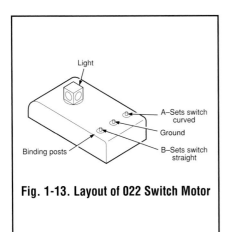

Fig. 1-13. Layout of 022 Switch Motor

A FLASHING EOT BOX

An end-of-train (EOT) box is a nice addition to the up-to-date layout and requires only the simplest wiring. Two versions are presented here. The first uses a flashing LED, a small lithium battery, and a slide switch. The second uses a commercial flasher module originally intended to light up clothing. Both are portable and can be installed on any car with a steel underbody in a matter of minutes.

PREPARE THE PARTS

Cut out the EOT box. The EOT box is made from a section of window stop. Although this piece of wood is nominally $\frac{1}{2}$" x $\frac{3}{4}$", it actually measures $\frac{7}{16}$" x $1\frac{1}{16}$". Since it may take several attempts to get the box right, a foot or more of window stop is recommended for this pro-

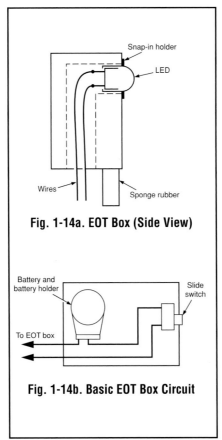

Fig. 1-14a. EOT Box (Side View)

Fig. 1-14b. Basic EOT Box Circuit

ject. With the razor saw and miter box (or other tools), measure and cut a $\frac{7}{16}$" piece from the end. Sand its ends smooth.

Next drill holes for the LED and its wiring. With a push pin, make a mark in the center of the box, about $\frac{1}{4}$" from the top. Then, at the mark, drill a $\frac{1}{4}$" hole about three-quarters through the box.

If you don't have a drill press or other heavy-duty tools, start with a small hole and gradually enlarge it. You will probably have to enlarge the hole beyond $\frac{1}{4}$". If you don't have anything larger, you can still use the $\frac{1}{4}$" bit to enlarge the hole by moving the bit around the edge. Next, drill a $\frac{1}{8}$" or $\frac{5}{32}$" hole in the bottom of the box, meeting the first hole at right angles. See fig. 1-14a.

Prepare the LED. Solder 2" of 26 gauge wire to the cathode of the LED (the longer lead, near the flat part of the case), and $2\frac{1}{2}$" inches to the anode.

Strip $\frac{1}{2}$" from the ends of each wire. Coil one end of each wire with the small paper clip. Clamp each LED in the Helping Hands. Slide each wire onto its respective lead until it is about $\frac{1}{16}$" from the LED. Because this joint is so close to the case, it is especially important to use the soldering heatsink to protect the LED from heat damage. Solder the joints, and trim the excess lead from the LED. Slide about $\frac{1}{2}$" of $\frac{1}{16}$" heat-shrink tubing over one solder joint, all the way up to the case, and use the hair dryer to shrink it in place.

Next snap the LED into its plastic holder, and feed the wires through the EOT box, from the top hole down. Pull the wires all the way through, and try to get the LED and its holder to fit into the top hole. You may have to enlarge one or both holes until the LED fits.

PARTS, MATERIALS, AND TOOLS

Parts

About a foot of ½" x ¾" window stop. Get this at the lumberyard or home supply.

Red blinking LED (276-036). This LED has all necessary electronic circuitry built in and does not need a current-limiting resistor.

Snap-in holder for T-1¾ LEDs (276-079)

SPST submini slide switch (275-406)

Lithium battery holder (270-430)

Lithium battery (CR2025, Duracell DL2025, Eveready ECR 2025, or similar battery that will fit the battery holder)

Two ceramic magnets about 1" x ¾" (64-1879)

Materials

Plastic tray from a microwave dinner, preferably one not divided into compartments

Silicone sealant (64-2314)

CA glue or other instant bonding glue (64-2308)

26 gauge black stranded wire. Not sold as such by Radio Shack, but can be removed from modular phone cord (278-365). Use a wire stripper to remove the plastic sheathing and get to the wires.

22 gauge black stranded wire (278-1218)

1/16" heat-shrink tubing (278-1627)

Black paint and primer

A few inches of black sponge rubber weather-stripping, approximately ½" square

.032 rosin-core solder (64-005)

Damp sponge

Medium-grade sandpaper

Small piece of stiff 22 or 24 gauge steel wire (optional)

Tools

Small metal miter box

Razor saw

Drill and bits ranging from ⅛" to 17/64"

Other tools: the same as those required for the simple LED circuit

---

When you are satisfied that it fits, test it with the lithium battery. Touch the wires to the battery poles. One side is positive and marked with a plus, while the other is negative and unmarked. If the LED flashes, you can remove the LED, the plastic holder, and the wires from the EOT box. If the LED fails to flash, switch the wires and try again. If you wish to do so, you can bend a piece of stiff wire into the shape of a handle and attach it to the top of the EOT box.

Paint the EOT box. Prime and paint the box. When it is dry, re-install the LED assembly and wires.

Attach the sponge rubber mount. The EOT box is secured to the coupler of a freight car by a black sponge rubber mount, which the coupler squeezes in place. Cut a piece of sponge rubber approximately ⅜" x ⅜" x ¼". Make a hole in the ¼" x ⅜" side with the small paper clip, and feed the wires through the hole. Attach this piece to the bottom of the EOT box with CA glue.

Now install the EOT box by inserting the mount into the coupler and closing it, as shown in fig. 1-15. You may have to trim the sponge rubber and fuss with it to get it to fit properly. If there isn't enough rubber, you can glue small pieces on. After you are satisfied that the EOT box fits, release it by opening the coupler. If the car has a nonoperating coupler, you may need a small screwdriver to force the rubber mount into place.

Prepare the battery holder. Examine the battery holder. The coin-shaped lithium battery slips in under the plastic tab marked with a plus sign. Two metal fingers contact the edge of the battery, which is part of the positive terminal. Turn the battery holder over. There should be three solder pins. The two on the left go to the positive terminal, while the one on the right goes to the negative terminal. The metal tab in the middle also goes to the negative terminal.

Trim the three solder pins, and bend the stubs out of the way. Find the positive terminal with its two contact fingers. Clamp the battery holder in the Helping Hands, and tin a small area on one side of the positive terminal, next to the contact

finger. Next tin one end of a 5" piece of 22 gauge stranded wire, and solder the wire to the area on the positive terminal that you just worked on. You can hold the wire in place with a piece of matchstick and tack it with the soldering pencil. Additional solder should not be necessary. Work quickly, so that you won't damage the plastic. Now solder a 2" piece of 22 gauge stranded wire to the negative terminal, on the other side in the center of the metal tab.

Mount the switch, battery holder, and magnets. See fig. 1-14b. From a microwave dinner tray, cut out a rectangle of plastic approximately 1½" x 2¼". Mount the magnets on one side of the rectangle with silicone sealant, one at each end. Next mount the battery holder and switch on the other side. Apply the sealant to the three small legs on the bottom of the battery holder and mount it at one end of the plastic rectangle. Then mount the slide switch on its side, at the

Fig. 1-15. EOT Box Installed on Boxcar Coupler

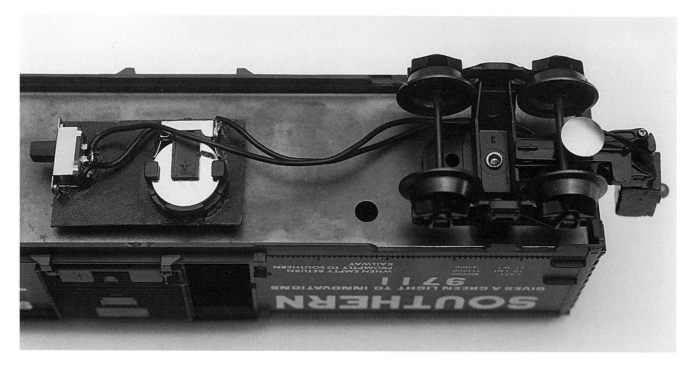

Fig. 1-16. Underside of Boxcar Showing EOT Wiring, with Slide Switch and Battery

other end. Make sure that the two terminals are away from the plastic, so that you can attach the wires easily. Allow the silicone sealant to set overnight.

WIRE AND INSTALL THE CIRCUIT

Wire the circuit. Solder the 2" wire from the battery holder to one terminal of the slide switch. Then solder a 5" piece of 22 gauge stranded wire to the second terminal of the slide switch. Strip the ends of both 5" wires, and splice them temporarily to the two wires coming from the EOT box. Insert the battery in its holder, the plus side facing up.

Move the slide switch handle back and forth. If the LED flashes, you can solder the joints. If not, the polarity is probably incorrect. Switch the wires from the EOT box with each other and try again. If the LED still doesn't flash, there is probably a break in the circuit, and you may have to take the EOT box apart to find it.

Label the wires that you spliced temporarily, so that you will know which wire goes to which. Slip a ¾" length of heat-shrink tubing on each wire from the EOT box, and solder the wires. Then push the heat-shrink tubing over the joints and shrink it in place with the hair dryer.

Install the circuit. Following fig. 1-16, attach the switch and battery holder assembly to the car bottom using the magnets, and guide the wires around the truck. Now install the EOT box in the coupler, as described on page 17. Dress the wires so that the truck turns freely without disturbing the EOT box. Make sure that the wires do not rub against the axles or wheels.

When you have to replace the battery, gently pry it up and out with a small screwdriver.

AN EOT BOX USING A COMMERCIAL FLASHER CIRCUIT

Commercial LED flasher circuits are available to light up clothing, toys, and other items. Each circuit consists of a circuit board containing batteries, a slide switch, and flashing circuitry. Commercial circuits can be adapted to power EOT boxes.

Generally the only additional items necessary are the EOT box with its LED and a current-limiting resistor.

The circuit described below is sold at discount houses under the trade name of Lightables. It consists of a circuit board to which 10 LEDs are attached. Other similar circuits may also be available.

PREPARE THE EOT BOX

Preparation of the EOT box and its wires is identical to that described in the preceding section. Each lead of the LED is attached to a 2" 26 gauge wire, which in turn is connected to a 5" 22 gauge wire.

ASSEMBLY

Modify and mount the circuit board. Referring to fig. 1-17, cut off the wires going to all but one LED, and trim them down to the circuit board. From a microwave dinner tray, cut out a plastic rectangle 1½" x 2¼" and mount the circuit board on it with silicone sealant. Leave a strip on the rectangle to the left, about ½" wide. Mount the magnets on the other side, one at each end. Trim the wires to the remaining LED to about 1¼", and strip the ends. Trim the leads of the 390-ohm resistor to about ⅜", and solder one lead to one wire coming from the circuit board. Finally, mount the resistor on the plastic with silicone sealant.

Wire the circuit. Test the unit before you solder it, in order to

make sure that the polarities are correct. Connect one 5" wire from the EOT box to the other resistor lead. Then connect the other 5" wire to the remaining wire on the module. If the unit flashes when

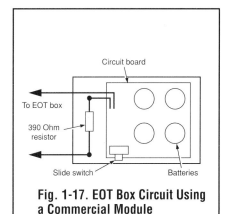

Fig. 1-17. EOT Box Circuit Using a Commercial Module

PARTS, MATERIALS, AND TOOLS

Lightables electric shirt module
Red T-1¾ LED (276-041). This is a standard, not a blinking, LED. You may be able to salvage one attached to the Lightables circuit board by carefully cutting away the plastic housing in which it is mounted.
390-ohm, .25-watt resistor (271-1114)

Other parts, materials, and tools:

The same as those required for the circuit described in the preceding section, except that the lithium battery, battery holder, and slide switch are omitted

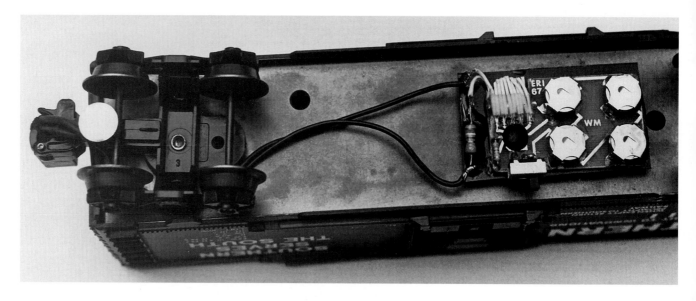

Fig. 1-18. EOT Circuit with a Commercial Module, Installed in Boxcar

you throw the slide switch, solder the joints. If it does not flash, switch the wires and try again.

Finally, attach the soldered joints to the plastic rectangle with silicone sealant.

Install the circuit. Installation of this circuit is identical to that in the preceding section. See fig. 1-18.

A PRESENCE DETECTOR AND A BLOCK POWER INDICATOR

Carl Weaver designed these simple LED circuits for use with Märklin trains. Because Märklin track, which supplies AC from studs in the ties, is electrically similar to three-rail tinplate track, it is easy to adapt these circuits to tinplate use.

PRESENCE DETECTOR

This circuit indicates the presence of a car or train in a block, even without track power. It is best suited for GarGraves and other track whose running rails are insulated from each other. As fig. 1-19 shows, one running rail in each block is insulated from neighboring blocks.

The LEDs, located on the control panel, have their own power supply and do not use track power. Any car or train with metal wheels connects the insulated rail to the ground rail and turns on an LED in the control panel.

Even if your layout uses standard sectional track, you can still enjoy the benefits of this circuit. In strategic locations, install individual sections of track, each with one insulated running rail. To insulate a running rail, insert plastic pins in each end, and cardboard strips between the rail and the metal ties. The cardboard from a matchbook or cereal box works well. Make sure that the rail does not touch the ties anywhere. (For more information on making track with insulated rails, see Peter Riddle's detailed discussion in *Greenberg's Wiring Your Lionel Layout, Vol. II: Intermediate Techniques*, pages 19–26.) You can also purchase track with insulated running rails.

Connect the insulated rail in each of these sections to the circuit (see fig. 1-20), and as the train makes its

---

MATERIALS LIST

Parts
One LED for each block
1-K, .25-watt resistor for each LED (271-1321)
IN4001 rectifier diode (276-1101)
22-µF or 47-µF 35-volt electrolytic capacitor
HO or N gauge power pack or 9-volt AC to DC adapter (273-1455). See the text.
One or more barrier strips, with as many positions as LEDs (274-659, 274-670, or 274-677)

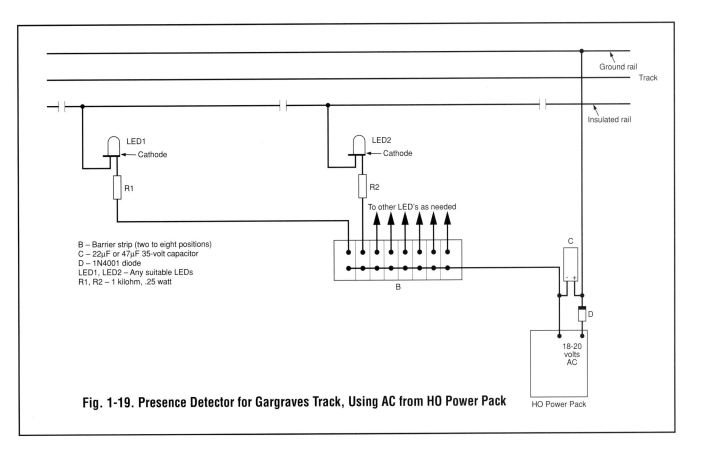

Fig. 1-19. Presence Detector for Gargraves Track, Using AC from HO Power Pack

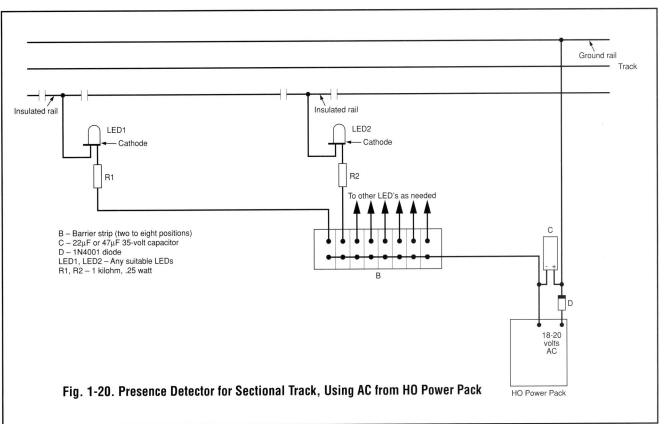

Fig. 1-20. Presence Detector for Sectional Track, Using AC from HO Power Pack

way around the layout, it will light up LEDs on the control panel.

There are several ways to power this circuit, each of which can supply approximately 20 LEDs. It is easiest to use the AC terminals of an HO power pack, as shown in figs. 1-19 and 1-20. To construct the presence detector:

❏ Solder the positive lead of the capacitor to the cathode lead of the 1-amp diode. This will reduce flickering caused by dirty track.

❏ Connect the anode of the diode to one AC terminal of the power pack.

❏ Connect the negative lead of the capacitor to the other AC terminal of the power pack.

❏ Solder a wire to the cathode of the diode and connect the other end to the ground, for example, an uninsulated outside rail.

❏ Solder the cathode of each LED to a 1-kilohm, .25-watt, current-limiting resistor.

❏ To each resistor, solder a wire to the second AC terminal of the power pack, the terminal to which the negative lead of the capacitor is connected. A barrier strip with a jumper across one row of terminals makes this job much easier. Connect one wire from the power pack to an end terminal on the barrier strip. Then install the jumper between that terminal and all the other terminals in the same row. While you can purchase a jumper strip specially designed for the purpose, a bare piece of 22 gauge solid wire will work just as well.

❏ Solder a wire from the anode of each LED to its section of insulated rail.

❏ Finally, snap each LED into each holder and then into its hole in the control panel.

You can also use the DC terminals of a power pack. The wiring is identical, except that 2.2-kilohm current-limiting resistors replace the 1-kilohm units. More resistance is necessary, because the diodes no longer block half the current, as they do with AC. If the LEDs do not go on when they should, flip the reversing switch, and the circuit should work.

If you don't have a power pack, you can use a 9-volt AC to DC

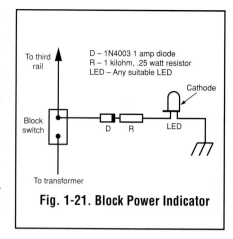

Fig. 1-21. Block Power Indicator

adapter (273-1455). Cut off the DC plug, strip the ends of the wires, and tin them. Equip each LED with a 1-kilohm resistor. If the LEDs do not work, switch the wires to the adapter.

BLOCK POWER INDICATOR

This device shows whether or not a block is receiving power. Referring to fig. 1-21, connect each LED, resistor, and diode to the ground and to the terminal on each block switch that feeds the third rail.

2

Automatic Stop Circuit

For many years Lionel offered stations and signals that automatically stopped trains and, after a brief interval, sent them on their way. The timing device used in these accessories, a wire heating element wound around a bimetallic thermostatic strip, closed a set of contacts that powered a special section of track. Normally, these contacts were open, and the section was dead, stopping any train that might enter. Once stopped, the train completed a circuit that turned on the heating element. Heat from the heating element gradually bent the thermostatic strip until the contacts closed, energizing the third rail and sending the train on its journey. Early versions of this device completed the circuit through an insulated running rail, while later versions did so through the third rail and the motor.

With a few common electronic parts, you can construct a stop circuit more reliable and flexible than Lionel's original device. With it, you can make trains stop automatically at any station or signal.

WHAT THE PARTS DO IN THE CIRCUIT

The circuit has nine electronic components: a 1.5-amp bridge rectifier, a 220-microfarad capacitor, a 4700-microfarad capacitor, a 12-volt, 1-amp voltage regulator, a 3.3-kilohm, .5-watt resistor, a 50-kilohm linear taper potentiometer ("pot" for short) or a 47-kilohm trimmer pot, a Darlington power translator, a 914/4148 diode, and a 12-volt SPDT relay with 10-amp contacts.

The *bridge rectifier* converts AC into DC, which is what the circuit requires. There are four wires or leads coming out of it. On the top, opposite one lead, there is a plus sign. This marks the *positive DC lead,* which is also longer than the others. From the positive lead it is possible to determine what everything else is. Diagonally opposite the positive lead is the *negative DC lead.* The remaining two leads are for the AC input. Since you are going to trim the leads and mount the device upside down, some other means of identifying the positive lead is necessary. The easiest procedure is to scratch a mark on the side of the rectifier below the plus sign. This rectifier is rated at 1.4 amps. This is the maximum amount of current it can carry.

Current comes out of the rectifier in pulses, 120 times a second. The circuit, however, needs current that flows in a steady stream, like that of a battery. That is what the 220-microfarad capacitor is for.

A *capacitor* is simply a tank for electrons. The size of the tank is measured in *farads.* Most capacitors are rated in *microfarads* (millionths of a farad, abbreviated µF) or even *picofarads* (millionths of a microfarad, abbreviated pF). Each capacitor in this circuit is electrolytic. An electrolytic capacitor uses an internal chemical compound in its operation and is polarized. Like an LED, it has a positive and a negative pole and must be connected properly. The negative pole is identified by one or more minus signs on the side of the device.

It is helpful to think of the direct current as entering the 220-microfarad capacitor as a series of pulses and emerging as a smooth flow. The current is then said to be filtered, and the capacitor is called a *filter capacitor.*

The *voltage regulator* is an integrated circuit that further smooths out the current and keeps the voltage at 12 volts. Excess voltage is eliminated as heat, which is carried away by the heatsink before it causes problems.

The 4700-microfarad capacitor, the 3.3-kilohm resistor, and the 47-kilohm (or 50-kilohm) potentiometer (or pot) make up the portion of the circuit that determines how long the train will be stopped.

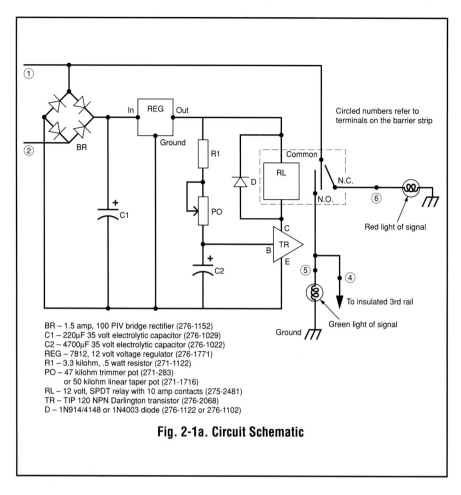

BR – 1.5 amp, 100 PIV bridge rectifier (276-1152)
C1 – 220μF 35 volt electrolytic capacitor (276-1029)
C2 – 4700μF 35 volt electrolytic capacitor (276-1022)
REG – 7812, 12 volt voltage regulator (276-1771)
R1 – 3.3 kilohm, .5 watt resistor (271-1122)
PO – 47 kilohm trimmer pot (271-283)
    or 50 kilohm linear taper pot (271-1716)
RL – 12 volt, SPDT relay with 10 amp contacts (275-2481)
TR – TIP 120 NPN Darlington transistor (276-2068)
D – 1N914/4148 or 1N4003 diode (276-1122 or 276-1102)

Fig. 2-1a. Circuit Schematic

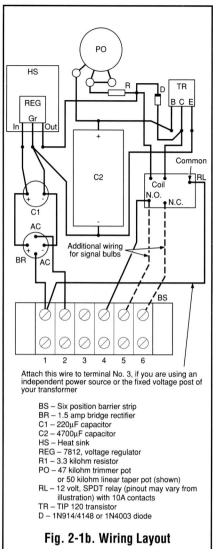

Attach this wire to terminal No. 3, if you are using an independent power source or the fixed voltage post of your transformer

BS – Six position barrier strip
BR – 1.5 amp bridge rectifier
C1 – 220μF capacitor
C2 – 4700μF capacitor
HS – Heat sink
REG – 7812, voltage regulator
R1 – 3.3 kilohm resistor
PO – 47 kilohm trimmer pot
    or 50 kilohm linear taper pot (shown)
RL – 12 volt, SPDT relay (pinout may vary from
    illustration) with 10A contacts
TR – TIP 120 transistor
D – 1N914/4148 or 1N4003 diode

Fig. 2-1b. Wiring Layout

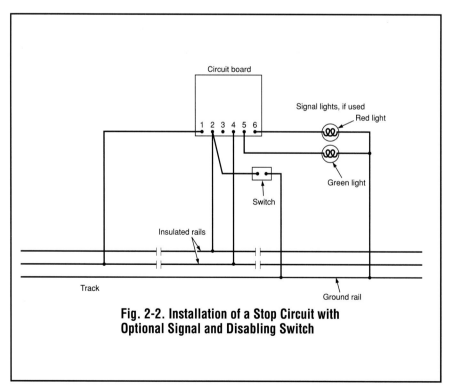

Fig. 2-2. Installation of a Stop Circuit with Optional Signal and Disabling Switch

Again, a capacitor is a tank for electrons. Now, it takes time to fill a tank and time to empty it. The amount of time it takes depends on the capacity of the tank and the size of the intake or discharge valve. This fact can be used to time events electronically. In this circuit, the 4700-microfarad capacitor is the timing tank, and the resistor and pot assembly are the valves. Valve size, or resistance, is measured in ohms. The pot acts like an adjustable valve with a resistance ranging from zero to about 50 kilohms. The 3.3-kilohm resistor acts as a fixed valve,

PARTS, MATERIALS, AND TOOLS

Electronic parts

Bridge rectifier, 100-volt, 1.4-amp (276-1152)

220-µF, 35-volt radial-lead electrolytic capacitor (272-1029)

4700-µF, 35-volt axial-lead electrolytic capacitor (272-1022)

3.3-K, .5-watt resistor (271-1122)

47-K trimmer potentiometer (271-283) or a 50-K, linear taper pot (271-1716). If you use the larger 50-K pot, you will also need a knob (e.g., 274-433).

TIP 120 NPN Darlington, power transistor (276-2068). A TIP 121 or TIP 142 device will also work. Do not use a PNP transistor.

7812 12-volt voltage regulator (276-1771)

IN914/4148 diode (276-1122) Or you can use an IN4003 diode (276-1102)

Mini 10-amp SPDT relay with 12-volt coil (275-248)

SPST (single pole, single throw) switch. This is a simple off-on switch. Any low-amperage toggle switch (e.g., 275-624) will do.

Other parts and materials

TO-220 heatsink (276-1363)

½" 4-40 machine screw with nut and lock washer, or use the TO 220 mounting kit (276-1373)

Silicone heatsink grease (276-1372)

Silicone rubber sealant (64-2314)

24 gauge solid wire (278-857 or 278-1509). You can use Radio Shack's two-conductor speaker wire (278-1509), consisting of two 24 gauge solid wires that can be pulled apart. Another possibility is Radio Shack's two-conductor 24 gauge intercom wire (278-857). Single-conductor 24 gauge solid wire is available from Digi-Key (C2003B-100-ND).

20 or 22 gauge solid wire (278-1216 or 278-1215)

Four- or six-position barrier strip (274-658 or 274-659). A six-position barrier strip is necessary if you are going to use the circuit to control a signal. Otherwise, use a four-position strip.

Two-position barrier strip (274-656) for the panel-mounted pot. See text.

.032" rosin-core solder (64-005). Do not use acid-core solder. It will corrode the joints.

Plastic tray from a microwave dinner, about 5" x 8", without separate compartments. Look for the PETE 1 logo in a triangle on the bottom. Plastic lids, such as those from margarine tubs, will not work, as silicone sealant will not adhere to them. You can mount the circuit on a piece of wood or another type of plastic. But first make sure that silicone sealant will adhere to it. Place a dab of sealant on it, and let it cure overnight. Then try to pull the sealant off.

Medium-grade sandpaper

Numbers from a videotape label. Radio Shack sells them without the videotapes (44-1103)

Damp sponge. A natural sponge is best.

Small (1¼") paper clip with one end straightened

Large (2") plastic-coated paper clip with one end straightened

1/16" or 3/32" heat-shrink tubing (278-1627)

Tools

15- to 30-watt soldering pencil/iron (64-2055, 64-2051, 64-2067, or 64-2070)

Soldering heatsink (276-1567). Not to be confused with the heatsink on which the voltage regulator will be mounted

Medium-size slotted screwdriver

Small (1/8" blade) slotted screwdriver

Needle-nose pliers (64-1812 or 64-1844)

Flat-nose or electrician's pliers (64-1871)

Wire stripper/cutter (64-1952 or 64-2129)

Helping Hands (64-2093) or similar project holder

Hacksaw or hobby tool with cutting disks, if you use the larger linear taper pot

Safety goggles, for cutting the shaft of the linear taper pot

Fig. 2-3. Voltage Regulator and Heatsink

Fig. 2-4. Transistor with Terminal Bent at Right Angles

current gain. The small control current is applied through the left terminal, called the *base,* and the larger operating current passes through the other two terminals, known respectively as the *collector* and the *emitter.* If there is no control current flowing into the base, no operating current can flow through the collector and the emitter, and the transistor is turned off. This transistor, because of its construction and the direction of its current flow (from base to emitter and from collector to emitter) is known as an NPN device.

Like the transistor, the *relay* enables a small flow of current (25 to 38 milliamps) to control a much larger flow (up to 10 amps). The relay keeps both currents isolated from each other, something that is not possible with a transistor. Housed in a sealed case, the relay consists of an electromagnet that closes one set of contacts and opens another. This contact arrangement makes it easy to turn a red signal off and a green signal on, the moment the relay energizes the third rail.

The 914/4148 diode protects the transistor and capacitors from back emf generated by the relay coil when its current is abruptly turned off. The diode short-circuits this momentary high voltage away from the components it could damage.

Figures 2-1a and 2-1b are the schematic and wiring layouts for this circuit. Figure 2-2 shows how the timing network controls the train. When the train pulls into the special track, it stops because the third rail is dead. Once stopped, its wheels and axles connect the insulated running rail to the ground, turning on the timing circuit. The timing circuit then starts charging the 4700-microfarad capacitor through the pot and the resistor. As long as this capacitor is being charged, no current gets to the

protecting the transistor from overload when the pot is set at zero ohms. Instead of filling and emptying tanks, we normally speak of charging and discharging the capacitor, and we call this type of arrangement a *resistance capacitance* or *RC circuit.*

The *transistor* is the electronic equivalent of a lever and enables a very small flow of current (for example, milliamps) to control a much larger flow (for example, amps). This particular device, called a Darlington, actually consists of two transistors, one driving the other.

This arrangement greatly increases the leverage effect of the transistor, known as its *beta,* or base of the transistor. As a result, no current flows through the collector and emitter, and the relay is turned off. Because the relay is turned off, no power gets to the third rail, and the train remains stopped. As soon as the capacitor is completely charged, however, the current has nowhere to go but into the base of the transistor, turning the transistor on and energizing the relay. The relay then closes the contacts that feed power to the third rail, sending the train on its way. The resistance of the pot determines the time it takes to charge the capacitor. Adjusting the pot increases or decreases its resistance and thus lengthens or shortens the interval during which the train is idle. Five to ten seconds after the train leaves the special section of track, the capacitor loses most of its charge and is ready for another cycle.

PREPARE AND MOUNT THE PARTS

Mount the voltage regulator and heatsink. See fig. 2-3. First, make sure that you are indeed working on the voltage regulator, and not the transistor. Both devices come in TO-220 cases, and it is easy to confuse then. The case of the voltage regulator should have the number "7812" printed on it, while that of the transistor should read "TIP 120," "TIP 121" or something similar. Smear a thin coating of silicone heatsink grease (not sealant) on the back of the voltage regulator. Place the voltage regulator in the heatsink over the hole so that its three terminals are facing toward you and the hole in the heatsink is away from you. Push the ½" 4-40 machine screw through the back of the heatsink and the voltage regulator tab. Install the lock washer and locknut. Tighten the locknut and screw with a small screwdriver and pliers. Now, with the pliers, bend the three

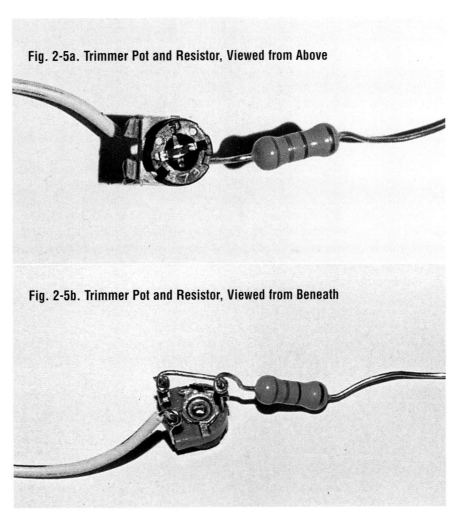

Fig. 2-5a. Trimmer Pot and Resistor, Viewed from Above

Fig. 2-5b. Trimmer Pot and Resistor, Viewed from Beneath

terminals at right angles, about ¼" from the case, so that the terminals face up.

If you use a TO-220 mounting kit, first smear a thin layer of silicone heatsink grease on both sides of the mica insulator and place it between the voltage regulator and the heatsink, fitting the hole in the mica over the hole in the heatsink. Before you install the machine screw, insert the plastic bushing in the hole on the heatsink. The bushing and mica sheet insulate the voltage regulator from the heatsink. Without them, the heatsink is electrically connected to the ground of the voltage regulator through the metal case. The bushing and mica sheet are not absolutely necessary. But if you do

not use them, make sure that nothing metal touches the heatsink.

Prepare the transistor. Referring to fig. 2-4, bend the terminals of the transistor at right angles, the same way you bent the terminals of the voltage regulator.

Prepare the pot and resistor assembly. You have two alternatives: either a trimmer pot or a larger linear taper pot with a knob.

Trimmer pot. A trimmer is a small pot mounted within a circuit. Figs. 2-5a and 2-5b show front and rear views of this device. Trimmers are meant to be adjusted initially and only occasionally thereafter. A trimmer pot does not require any cutting or extra parts but is a bit inconvenient to use, since a small screwdriver is needed to adjust it.

If you don't particularly like cutting metal but are willing to tolerate a little inconvenience, you may prefer the trimmer pot.

Take a moment to examine the trimmer pot. The adjustment knob has a slot for a screwdriver, although you may be able to turn it with your fingers. Turn the pot over, and look at the terminals. The two terminals on the straight edge are connected to each end of a resistor while the third, on the curved edge, is connected to a wiper that sweeps across the resistor, varying its resistance.

Prepare the trimmer pot and the 3.3-kilohm resistor as follows:

❑ Use the large straightened paper clip to make a loop consisting of two or three closely spaced turns in the end of one resistor lead.

❑ About ⅜" from the first loop, use the paper clip to make a second loop, consisting of one turn.

❑ Clamp the pot in the Helping Hands upside down with the straight edge facing you. The three terminals should be facing up.

❑ Push the two loops onto the two terminals. Note that one loop goes to the terminal on the curved edge, while the other goes to the lower left terminal on the straight edge. Use the needle-nose pliers to squeeze the loops tight around the terminals.

❑ Solder each loop to its terminal.

❑ Cut a 4" length of 24 gauge wire and strip ½" from each end.

❑ Use the paper clip to make a loop consisting of two or three closely spaced turns in one end of the wire.

❑ Push the loop onto the remaining terminal of the pot and squeeze it tight with the needle-nose pliers.

❑ Solder the third loop in place.

Linear taper pot with knob. The larger linear taper pot (see fig. 2-6) takes some extra work to install. However, it is more rugged than the trimmer pot and, once installed, easier to adjust.

The linear taper pot can also be mounted right on your control panel, within easy reach. If you choose this arrangement, mount a two-position barrier strip on the circuit board where the pot would have been. Then wire it according to fig. 2-7.

First examine the pot. Look at its three terminals. They correspond to the three terminals on the trimmer pot. The two end terminals are connected to the ends of a carbon resistor, while the center terminal is connected to a wiper that sweeps across the resistor. The shaft turns the wiper varying the resistance of the device. The device is called "linear" because its resistance varies directly with the rotation of the shaft and can be represented as a straight line on a graph.

Prepare the linear taper pot as follows, referring to fig. 2-8.

❑ With a hacksaw or hobby tool, cut the shaft down to about ½"

❑ Clamp the pot in the Helping Hands so that the shaft faces down and the three terminals face you.

❑ Pass a lead of the 3.3-kilohm resistor through the hole in the center terminal of the pot.

❑ Bend the end of the lead in a small V and hook it onto the left-hand terminal. Squeeze the lead with the needle-nose pliers so that it is firmly in place and solder it to the left-hand terminal.

❑ Solder the same lead to the center terminal after making sure that the lead is pressed firmly against it. Squeeze or bend it with the needle-nose pliers to secure it if necessary.

❑ Cut a 4" length of 24 gauge wire for the right-hand terminal and strip ½" off the ends.

❑ Solder the 4" wire to the right-hand terminal.

❑ Remove the pot from the Helping Hands, and install the knob on the shaft: Loosen the set screw (in the side of the knob) with a small screwdriver. Then push the knob onto the shaft, and tighten the set screw.

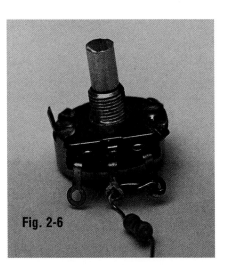

Fig. 2-6

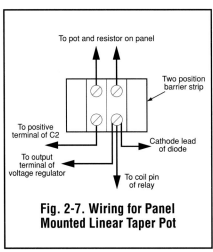

To pot and resistor on panel

Two position barrier strip

To positive terminal of C2

To output terminal of voltage regulator

Cathode lead of diode

To coil pin of relay

Fig. 2-7. Wiring for Panel Mounted Linear Taper Pot

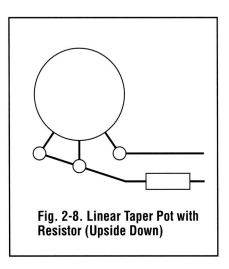

Fig. 2-8. Linear Taper Pot with Resistor (Upside Down)

Wire the relay. Because of the location of its pins, the relay, unlike the other parts, must be wired before it is mounted.

The relay comes with a pinout or diagram that tells what each pin is for. Usually the pinout is on the package or a separate sheet, but sometimes it is printed on the relay case itself. Relays do not have standard pin arrangements, and as a result, pinouts differ according to manufacturer.

Examine the relay, and match its pins to those on the pinout. There are five pins. Two labeled "coil," go to the electromagnet that operates the device. The remaining three pins go to the contacts that carry the track and signal current. One is labeled "Common" and feeds both sets of contacts. The other two are labeled "normally open" (N.O.) and "normally closed" (N.C.) respectively. "Normally" means "when the relay is not energized." When the relay is energized, the normally open contacts are closed and the normally closed contacts are opened.

Refer to the circuit layout in fig. 2-1b to get an idea of how long the wires should be. The diagram is for a circuit that operates a two-position signal, in addition to stopping the train. If you are not going to install a signal, omit the wires represented by dotted lines. You can then use a four-position barrier strip instead of the six-position unit illustrated.

Following the circuit layout in fig. 2-1b, cut the five wires to size, making allowance for the extra lengths needed for connections. A little too long is better than a little too short. The two wires to the coil pins can be 24 gauge, but the three wires to the relay contacts, which carry track power, should be 20 or 22 gauge. Strip ½" from each end of each wire. With the large paper clip, coil one end of each of the wires that will go to the relay

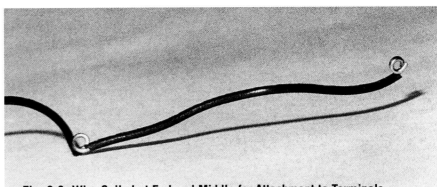

Fig. 2-9. Wire Coiled at End and Middle for Attachment to Terminals

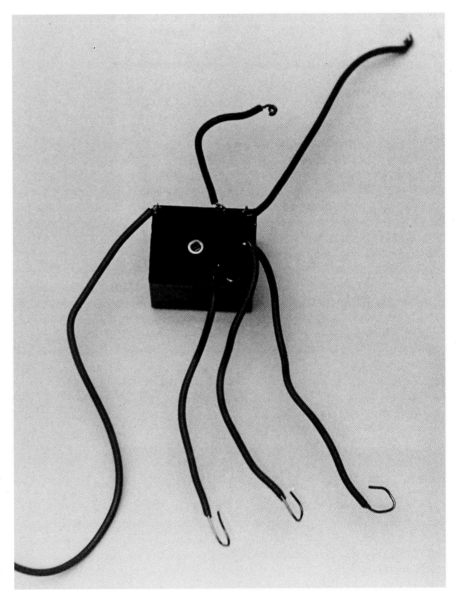

2-10. Relay with Wires Soldered, Viewed from Beneath

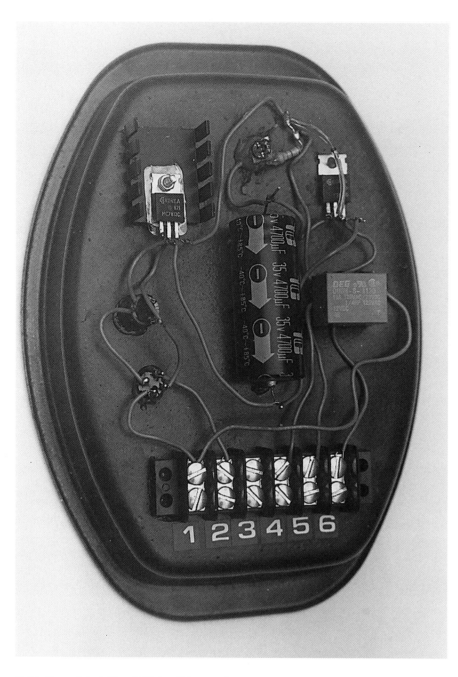

2-11. Completed Circuit Using Trimmer Pot

contacts, that is, to the N.O., N.C., and Common pins.

If you are using the circuit to operate a signal, you can take a shortcut when you wire the N.O. pin. This pin, like several connections in this circuit, has more than one wire going to it. It is possible to coil the ends of two separate pieces of wire with the large paper clip, and to attach them both to the terminal. But there is an easier way. You can combine the two parts of the connection by using just one wire with a ⅜" stripped section in the middle. You can then coil that section of wire on the large paper clip and attach it just like an end section (see fig. 2-9). When you calculate the amount of wire you

need, add ½" for each solder joint and ½" for each terminal connection. Stripping insulation from the middle of the wire is a little tricky, because if you wield the wire stripper too vigorously, you can push all the insulation off one end.

Place the relay upside down on your work surface. Attach one alligator clip from the Helping Hands to a pin to keep the relay from moving. Now, push the coiled end (or middle section, as noted above) of each wire onto its pin. With the needle-nose pliers, squeeze the loops onto their pins. Then solder them in place. After you have soldered the four exposed pins, you can attach the alligator clip to one of them and solder the fifth pin. Label the wires with strips of tape, so that you will know what pins they are connected to.

Miscellaneous items. Trim the terminals of the capacitors and the rectifier down to ½". Finally, scratch a mark on the side of the rectifier case near the positive (+) terminal.

Mount the parts. While it is possible to mount the circuit on a piece of hardboard (the textbook way), it is easier and cheaper to use plastic from a microwave dinner tray. This type of plastic, while not as rigid as hardboard, will do the job and is a lot easier to find.

It is easiest simply to mount the circuit on the bottom of an inverted tray. For convenient locations to mount parts on the tray, see figs. 2-1b, 2-11, and 2-12. Before you mount the barrier strip or strips, loosen all the screws. It is much easier to do this now than afterwards. Leave plenty of room for attaching the wires, and make sure that the relay is oriented properly. Attach the parts with the silicone sealant except for the diode. If you are using a trimmer pot, be careful that no sealant gets inside the device or prevents the adjustment screw from turning. Let everything cure overnight. With the numbers from the videotape label, number the terminals from one to six.

WIRE THE CIRCUIT

Figure 2-la shows the circuit schematic, while fig. 2-1b shows the actual wiring layout.

For the rest of the circuit, use 24 gauge solid wire. Plug in the soldering pencil. While it is heating, you can start wiring the circuit.

❏ Screw the N.O. and N.C. wires from the relay contacts into the barrier strip. The two wires from the N.O. pin go to terminals 4 and 5 on the barrier strip. If you require only one wire from the N.O. terminal (see the previous section), connect it to terminal 4. The wire from the N.C. pin goes to terminal 6. For each connection, remove the screw, and wrap the end of the wire around it clockwise. Then use the wire to lower the screw into its hole and screw it back in.

❏ Attach one wire to an AC terminal of the rectifier. Cut a piece of wire long enough to go from one AC rectifier lead to terminal 1 (the left terminal) of the barrier strip with about 1¼" to spare. Strip about ½" from each end. Lightly sand the wire, coil one end with the small paper clip, and push it onto an AC rectifier lead. Push the wire down until it is about ⅛" above the rectifier itself. If the wire is loose, squeeze it tight with the needle-nose pliers.

❏ Solder this wire to the rectifier. Clamp the circuit board to the Helping Hands to keep it from moving. Attach the soldering heat-sink to the rectifier lead between the joint and the case, and solder the joint. Trim the excess portion of rectifier lead.

❏ Attach the other end of this wire to terminal 1 of the barrier strip, along with the Common wire from the relay. Wrap both wires around the screw and screw them in.

❏ Solder a wire to the second AC rectifier terminal. Then screw the

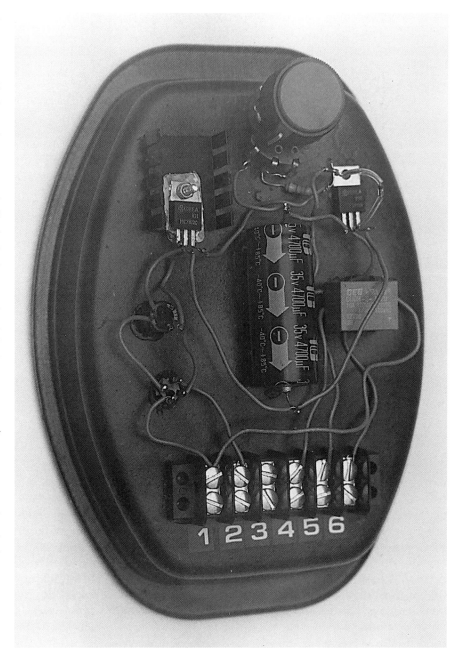

2-12. Completed Circuit Using Linear Taper Pot

other end of this wire into terminal 2 of the barrier strip.

❏ Solder a wire from the positive DC lead of the rectifier to the positive lead of the 220-microfarad capacitor, and from there to the input (left-hand) terminal of the voltage regulator. You should be able to identify the positive rectifier lead by the mark you made on the

side of the case. As with the N.O. connection to the relay (see the section labeled "wire the relay," above), you can use a single wire instead of two, if you strip a ⅜" section from the middle and coil it on the small paper clip.

❏ Solder the remaining wires. Refer to fig. 2-1b. The remaining connections, most of which lend

31

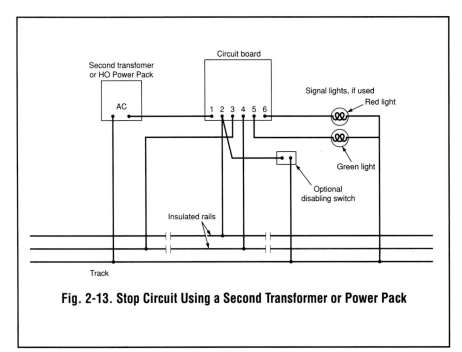

Fig. 2-13. Stop Circuit Using a Second Transformer or Power Pack

themselves to the procedure discussed in the preceding paragraph, are soldered in the same way. For each connection, first coil the ends or middle of the wire with the small paper clip. Be sure to use the soldering heatsink, especially with the transistor, bridge rectifier, and voltage regulator. These components are easily damaged by heat. These wires are connected as follows:

❏ From one coil connection of the relay to the collector (center terminal) of the transistor. Leave a little space on the transistor terminal for the diode, which will be attached later.

❏ From the other coil connection of the relay to the resistor. Leave a ⅜" length of lead from the resistor for attaching the diode and the wire to the voltage regulator output. If you have mounted the pot on your control panel, connect this wire to the lower right-hand screw on the two-position barrier strip.

❏ From the output (right-hand terminal) of the voltage regulator to the resistor. When you attach this wire, also attach the diode. It goes from the resistor to the collector

(center terminal) of the transistor, cathode (banded end) toward the resistor. Slip a piece of 1/16" heat-shrink tubing ½" long over each lead before you coil the ends and solder it. If you have a panel-mounted pot, this wire, the wire to one coil connection on the relay, and the lead from the cathode (banded end) of the diode all go to the lower right-hand screw of the two-position barrier strip. If you find it too awkward to attach the two wires and diode lead to the screw, first attach a short wire to the screw. Then solder the other wires and the diode lead to the short wire.

❏ From the negative DC lead of the rectifier to the negative lead of the 220-microfarad capacitor; then, to the ground connection (center terminal) of the voltage regulator; then to the negative terminal of the 4700-microfarad capacitor; finally to the emitter (right-hand terminal) of the transistor.

❏ From the pot to the positive lead of the 4700-microfarad capacitor, and then to the base (left-hand terminal) of the transistor. This is the

wire you had soldered to the pot earlier. If you have a panel-mounted pot, this wire starts with a connection to the lower left-hand screw of the two-position barrier strip.

TEST AND INSTALL THE CIRCUIT

Test the circuit. First check to see that all the connections and polarities are correct and also that neighboring solder joints do not touch each other. If the joints or leads are too close together, use the small screwdriver to push them apart. If you did not use a mica insulator, inspect the heatsink. Make sure that no stray wires touch the heatsink, since it is electrically connected to the negative (middle) terminal of the voltage regulator.

Then perform a quick test of the timing circuit. Connect one end of a wire to terminal 1 and the other end to a terminal on your transformer. Connect a second wire to terminal 2, but leave it free for the time being. Now turn the pot counterclockwise as far as it will go. Turn the power on, and touch the second wire to the other transformer terminal. In a second or two you should hear a click, which is the relay turning on. Remove the second wire from the transformer terminal. You should hear a second click as the relay disengages. Now wait about ten seconds, turn the pot clockwise about quarter of a turn, and repeat the test. The relay should take several seconds longer to come on. Repeat the test with different pot settings. You should be able to adjust the pot so that the relay can take up to a minute to turn on. Note, though, that if you adjust the pot to its highest setting, too little current may get through to turn the relay on at all.

At this point you can test the relay contacts for signal operation. Connect an additional wire to terminal 2 and attach it to the common or ground terminal of the signal, which is usually the center binding post. Connect wires from other two binding posts on the signal to terminals 5 and 6 on the barrier strip. The wire from the binding post connected to the green light goes to 5, while the wire from the binding post connected to the red light goes to 6. Repeat the test in the previous paragraph. The signal should show red at first and then, at the click, should change to green. If the lights go on in the wrong order, switch the wires to terminals 5 and 6.

Now disconnect the wire from terminal 5 and attach it to terminal 4, which will feed the insulated third rail. You should notice no difference when you run the test.

To test a circuit using the four-position terminal strip, connect a 12-volt bulb to terminal 2 and terminal 4. The bulb should go on when the relay clicks.

If anything is not working right, either neighboring joints or bare leads are touching, or there is a loose or open connection.

Prepare the track. This circuit requires a special section of track long enough to keep the train from coasting past when the power is off. If you are running a trolley line, one or two pieces of track may be enough. Otherwise a section three or four pieces long may be necessary.

The third rail of the special section must be insulated in order to stop the train. To insulate the third rail, replace the metal pin at each end with an insulating plastic pin. If you are certain that the track will not move, you can omit the plastic pin and use the air gap between the rails as insulation.

One running (outside) rail of the special section must also be insulated. Insulating a piece of running rail removes it from the circuit until a train passes over. When the train passes over, its wheels and

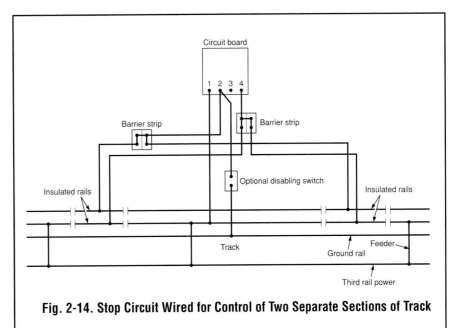

Fig. 2-14. Stop Circuit Wired for Control of Two Separate Sections of Track

axles ground the insulated rail through the other running rail, turning on the timing circuit. To insulate the running rail, replace the metal pins at each end with plastic pins, and insert thin cardboard or fiber strips between the rail and each metal tie. The rail must not touch a tie anywhere. To make sure that you have complete insulation, test the section as follows: Connect two wires to your transformer. Then touch the end of one wire to one running rail and the end of the other wire to the other running rail. You should not get a spark. If you do, find out where the break in the insulation is and correct it. Feel around the plastic pins and the cardboard strips. The break in the insulation will most likely feel warm to the touch. (For more information on making and using insulated rails, see Peter Riddle's detailed discussion in *Greenberg's Wiring Your Lionel Layout, Vol II: Intermediate Techniques*, pages 19–26.)

Install the circuit. Figure 2-2 shows how the circuit is installed on the layout. Terminals 5 and 6

can be connected to the green and red lights respectively of a two-position signal. The switch, which grounds terminal 2, disables the circuit, allowing the train to run through without stopping. To use it, first turn the pot counterclockwise all the way. Then turn the switch on. You should hear a click, and the green signal light, if any, should go on. The switch fools the circuit into thinking that there is a train on the track.

Fixed-voltage operation. The circuit is wired to operate on track voltage, but at very low voltages (below 8 volts), the relay might not turn on. To cure this problem, you can wire the circuit for fixed voltage from your transformer or from the AC terminals of an HO power pack. First, find the wire that goes from the Common pin of the relay to terminal 1. Then disconnect it from terminal 1, and attach it to terminal 3. Refer to figs. 2-1b and 2-13. Connect a wire from a live section of third rail (or from the power supply for the third rail) to terminal 3. Now connect one wire from the independent power source

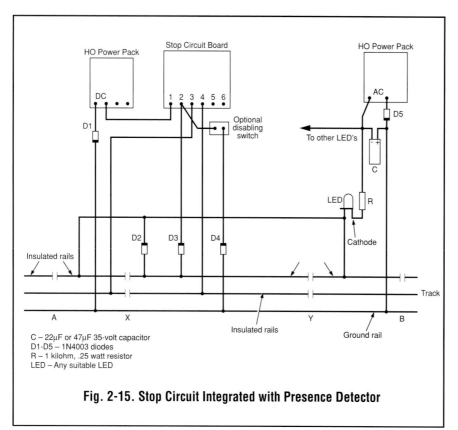

C – 22µF or 47µF 35-volt capacitor
D1-D5 – 1N4003 diodes
R – 1 kilohm, .25 watt resistor
LED – Any suitable LED

Fig. 2-15. Stop Circuit Integrated with Presence Detector

dently of one other, you will need to construct additional stop circuits.

Integrating the stop circuit and presence detector. Both the presence detector described in Chapter 1 and the stop circuit use an insulated running rail. Figure 2-15 shows how it is possible to integrate both circuits so that they will work together without interfering with each other. When a train is on section AX of Block AB, the LED is turned on, but diodes D1 and D2 block current from entering the stop circuit and activating it. Because the anodes of D2 and D3 oppose each other, current from one circuit cannot sneak into the other. When the train enters section XY, current through diode D2 continues to power the LED, while current though diode D3 turns on the stop circuit. As the train moves on to section YB, the LED continues to glow, and once again, diodes D1 and D2 keep current from the presence detector out of the stop circuit.

The stop circuit must be powered by the DC terminals of its own power pack, and diodes D1 through D5 installed as indicated. Otherwise, current from one circuit will find a sneak path into the other. This arrangement cannot use track voltage or fixed voltage from the same transformer that powers the track. If the stop circuit refuses to work, flip the reversing switch on the power pack.

to terminal 1 and a second wire from the same power source to the ground. If you are using the fixed-voltage post of your transformer, you can omit the second wire, since the transformer is already connected to the ground.

Control of multiple sections. As fig. 2-14 shows, the circuit can control two or more separate sections of track, a useful feature if you are running a trolley line with a number of stops. Notice that the circuit turns all the sections on simultaneously. This arrangement requires two additional barrier strips, each with as many positions as there are insulated sections of track. Make sure that each intervening block of track has its own third rail feeder. If you wish to control additional sections independ-

3

Circuits for Tinplate Highway Flashers and Signals

A CIRCUIT FOR THE 154/2154 HIGHWAY FLASHER

Throughout the accessory's existence, Lionel's 154/2154 highway flasher came with a 154C contactor, which produced irregular and unprototypical flashes. Only in recent years has Lionel offered a solid-state, prototypically operating flasher. But if you have one of the older units, don't despair. You can make it flash prototypically with a simple circuit using a handful of electronic components. (This circuit is based on one published by Peter Thorne in his book *34 New Electronic Projects for Model Railroaders* and has been modified with tinplate operation in mind.) The circuit will also operate Marx highway flashers.

THE PARTS AND WHAT THEY DO IN THE CIRCUIT

There are nine electronic components: a 1.4-amp bridge rectifier, a 470-microfarad capacitor, two 220-microfarad capacitors, a 12-volt, 1-amp voltage regulator, two 3.9-kilohm, .5-watt resistors, and two Darlington power transistors.

Most of these parts do the same things in this circuit as in the automatic stop circuit described in Chapter 2. The bridge rectifier converts AC into pulsating DC, which the 470-microfarad filter capacitor smooths out into a steady flow. The voltage regulator further smooths out the DC flow and keeps the voltage at 12 volts. Excess voltage is eliminated as heat, which the heatsink dissipates into the air. Each 220-microfarad capacitor, together with the accompanying 3.9-kilohm resistor forms an RC circuit that times the flashing of the signal. Each transistor acts like a lever, enabling a very small flow of current to control a much

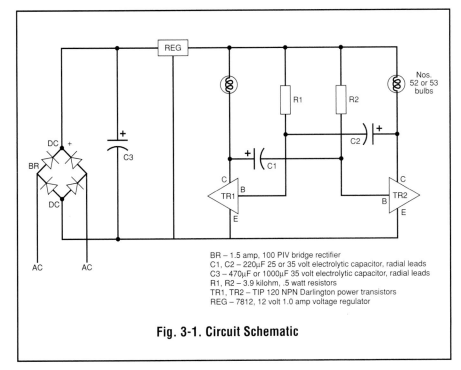

BR – 1.5 amp, 100 PIV bridge rectifier
C1, C2 – 220µF 25 or 35 volt electrolytic capacitor, radial leads
C3 – 470µF or 1000µF 35 volt electrolytic capacitor, radial leads
R1, R2 – 3.9 kilohm, .5 watt resistors
TR1, TR2 – TIP 120 NPN Darlington power transistors
REG – 7812, 12 volt 1.0 amp voltage regulator

Fig. 3-1. Circuit Schematic

larger flow. Because the circuit does not control track current, there is no need for a relay.

Figure 3-1 shows how the timing network and transistors are interconnected so as to turn the lights on and off alternately. When the left light is lit, current flows through transistor TR1. A small current flows into the base via resistor R1, turning the transistor on. As a result, a much larger current flows through the collector and the emitter, lighting the bulb. At the same time, the collector voltage of transistor TR1 charges capacitor C1 by pulling current into C1 via resistor R2. As long as this is happening, current is diverted into capacitor C1 and away from the base of transistor TR2. With no current entering into the base, TR2 and its light are turned off.

As soon as capacitor C1 is fully charged, however, the current has nowhere to go but into the base of transistor TR2, turning on TR2 and its light. Meanwhile, the collector voltage of TR2 charges capacitor C2 by pulling current into capacitor C2 via resistor R1. This diverts current from the base of transistor TR1. Since current can no longer get to the base of TR1, TR1 is turned off, and its light goes out. Without the voltage from the collector of TR1, capacitor C1 loses its charge. Transistor TR1 stays turned off until capacitor C2 is fully charged. At this point, the current has nowhere to go but into the base of transistor TR1. TR1 now turns back on, and the cycle starts all over again. With the components specified, the whole cycle takes about 1.2 seconds. The entire circuit is called a free-running multivibrator.

PARTS, MATERIALS, AND TOOLS
Electronic Parts
Bridge rectifier, 100-volt, 1.4-amp (276-1152)

One 470-µF, 25- or 35-volt radial-lead electrolytic capacitor (272-1030). You can also use a 1000-µF unit (272-1032)

Two 220-µF, 25- or 35-volt radial-lead electrolytic capacitors (272-1029)

Two 3.9-K, .5-watt resistors (271-1123)

Two TIP 120 NPN Darlington, power transistors (276-2068). You can also use a TIP 121, or TIP 142. Do not use a PNP transistor.

One 7812 voltage regulator (276-1771)

Other parts and materials

TO-220 heatsink (276-1363)

½" 4-40 machine screw with nut and lock washer. Or use a TO-220 mounting kit (276-1373).

Silicone heatsink grease (276-1372)

Silicone rubber sealant (64-2314)

24 gauge solid wire (278-1509 or 278-857). Radio Shack does not sell single-conductor 24 gauge solid wire. However, it does sell wire for speakers (278-1509) and intercoms (278-857) consisting of two insulated 24 gauge solid wires side by side. These wires can be pulled apart and used just like the single-conductor variety.

One 6-position barrier strip (274-659)

.032 rosin-core solder (64-005). Do not use acid-core solder.

Plastic tray from microwave dinner, about 5" x 8" without separate compartments. Look for the PETE 1 logo in a triangle on the bottom. The circuit will be mounted on this tray. You can use wood or another type of plastic, but first make sure that silicone sealant will stick to it.

No. 52 or no. 53 bulbs (272-1127 or 272-1117), if needed

Red aerosol spray paint from an auto supply store, if necessary, for spraying clear lightbulbs red

Medium-grade sandpaper

Numbers from a videotape label (44-1103)

Damp sponge

Piece of cardboard from a matchbook or a cereal box

Tools
15- to 30-watt soldering pencil/iron (64-2051 or 64-2067)

Soldering heatsink (276-1567). Not to be confused with the heatsink on which the voltage regulator will be mounted.

Medium-size screwdriver

Small (⅛") slotted screwdriver

Needle-nose pliers (64-1812 or 64-1844)

Flat-nose or electrician's pliers (64-1871)

Wire stripper/cutter (64-1952 or 64-2129)

Small (1.25") paper clip with one end straightened

Helping Hands (64-2093) or similar project holder

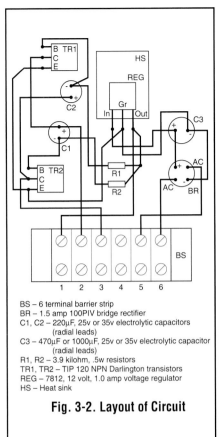

BS – 6 terminal barrier strip
BR – 1.5 amp 100PIV bridge rectifier
C1, C2 – 220μF, 25v or 35v electrolytic capacitors
    (radial leads)
C3 – 470μF or 1000μF, 25v or 35v electrolytic capacitor
    (radial leads)
R1, R2 – 3.9 kilohm, .5w resistors
TR1, TR2 – TIP 120 NPN Darlington transistors
REG – 7812, 12 volt, 1.0 amp voltage regulator
HS – Heat sink

Fig. 3-2. Layout of Circuit

Fig. 3-3. The Completed Flasher Circuit

PREPARE AND MOUNT THE PARTS

Preparation of parts is very similar to that of the automatic stop circuit described in Chapter 2.

Assemble the voltage regulator and heatsink. See fig. 2-3. Smear a thin coating of silicone heatsink grease (not sealant) on the back of the voltage regulator. Place the voltage regulator in the heatsink over the hole so that its three terminals face you and the hole in the heatsink is away from you. Push the ½" 4-40 machine screw through the back of the heatsink and the voltage regulator tab. Install the lock washer and locknut. Tighten the locknut and screw with a small screwdriver and pliers. Now with the flat-nose or electrician's pliers, bend the three terminals about ¼" from the ends at

right angles, so that they face up.

If you use the TO-220 mounting kit, smear a thin coating of heatsink grease on both sides of the mica sheet, and install it between the voltage regulator and the heatsink. Put the plastic bushing on the screw, narrow rim facing the heatsink, before you insert the screw in the heatsink. While not absolutely necessary, the bushing and the mica sheet insulate the heatsink from the case of the voltage regulator, which is a ground connection.

Prepare the transistors. Referring to fig. 2-4, bend up the terminals of each transistor, just as you did the terminals of the voltage regulator.

Prepare the capacitors and rectifier. Trim the terminals of the capacitors and the rectifier down to ½". Then scratch a mark on the

side of the rectifier case near the positive (+) terminal.

Mount the parts on the microwave dinner tray. You can mount the parts directly on an uncut microwave dinner tray, like the circuit in Chapter 2. Or you can mount them on a square of plastic cut from the tray, as shown in the photos. The circuit requires a square about 3½" on each side. Score the plastic with a utility knife, and then cut it with scissors. For convenient locations to mount parts on the plastic, see figs. 3-2 and 3-3. Leave enough room for attaching the wires. Loosen the screws on the barrier strip first. Then attach all the parts, except the resistors, with silicone sealant, and let everything cure overnight. With the numbers from the videotape label, number the terminals on the barrier strip one to six.

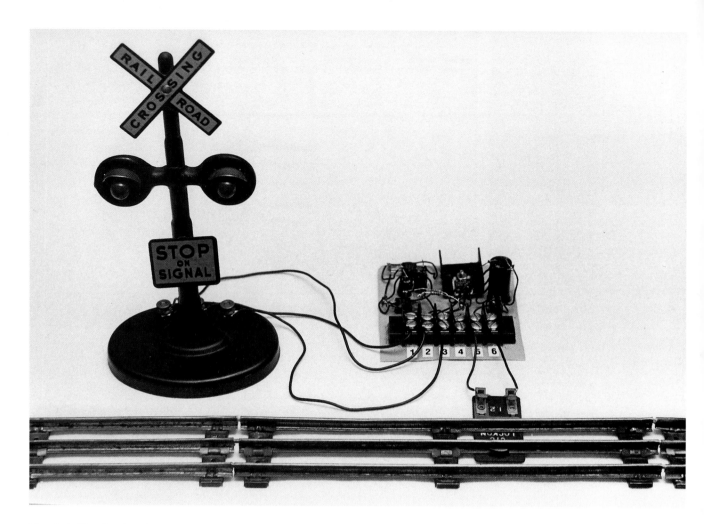

Fig. 3-4. The Flasher Circuit Powered by Track Voltage

WIRE THE CIRCUIT

Figure 3-1 shows the circuit schematic, while fig. 3-2 shows how the unit is actually wired.

First plug in the soldering pencil. While it is heating, you can start wiring the device.

❏ Prepare the first wire for soldering. Cut a piece of wire long enough to go from one AC rectifier lead to terminal 6 of the barrier strip (the right-hand terminal) with about 1¼" to spare. Strip about ½" from each end. Lightly sand the wire and wind two or three turns of the stripped end tightly around the straightened end of the paper clip. Trim off the excess and, with the needle-nose pliers, make sure that the wire end is pressed tightly against the paper clip and that the turns are close together. Remove the wire from the paper clip, and push it onto an AC rectifier lead until it is about ¼" above the rectifier. If the wire is loose, squeeze it tight with the needle-nose pliers. The other stripped end goes to terminal 6 of the barrier strip. Remove the screw and wrap the wire around it clockwise. Then use the wire to lower the screw in its hole and screw it back in.

❏ Clamp the circuit board to the Helping Hands.

❏ Clamp the soldering heatsink onto the rectifier lead between the joint and case.

❏ Solder the joint.

❏ Trim the excess rectifier lead.

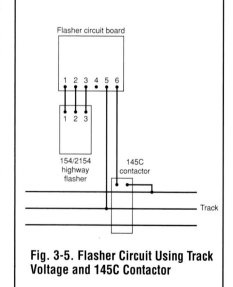

Fig. 3-5. Flasher Circuit Using Track Voltage and 145C Contactor

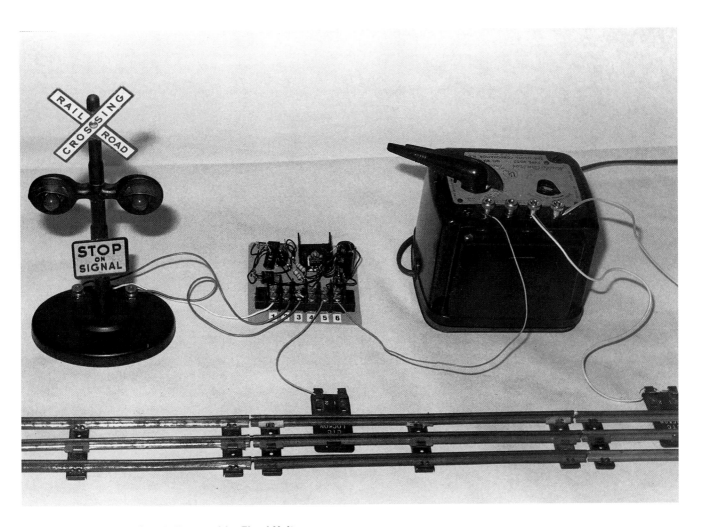

Fig. 3-6. The Flasher Circuit Powered by Fixed Voltage

❏ Solder a wire from terminal 5 of the barrier strip to the other AC rectifier lead, exactly as you soldered the first one.

❏ Solder a wire from the positive rectifier lead to the positive terminal of capacitor C3 and from there to the input (left-hand terminal) of the voltage regulator. For the connection to the capacitor terminal, strip ⅜" from the middle of the wire and coil it on the paper clip. Then attach it just like an end section. When you calculate the amount of wire you need, add ½" for each solder joint. Be careful not to push all the insulation off one end.

❏ Solder the remaining wires in the same way. Be sure to use the soldering heatsink, especially with the transistors, bridge rectifier, and voltage regulator. The remaining wires run:

❏ From the negative terminal of the rectifier to the negative terminal of capacitor C3; then to the ground (center terminal) of the voltage regulator; then to the emitter (right-hand terminal) of transistor TR2; and finally to the emitter (right-hand terminal) of transistor TR1.

❏ From the collector (center terminal) of transistor TR1 to the positive terminal of capacitor C1; then to terminal 2 on the barrier strip.

❏ From the positive terminal of the capacitor C2 to the collector (center terminal) of transistor TR2; then to terminal 3 of the barrier strip.

❏ From terminal 1 of the barrier strip to the output (right-hand terminal) of the voltage regulator; then to the junction with resistors R1 and R2. Do not attach the resistors or coil this end of the wire yet. Just strip the end of the wire, and leave it unattached for the moment.

❏ From the base (left-hand terminal) of transistor TR1 to the negative lead of capacitor C2 and then to resistor R1. Strip the end of this wire, but do not attach the resistor just yet.

❏ From the base (left-hand terminal) of transistor TR2 to the negative lead of capacitor C1 and then to resistor R2. Strip the end of this wire, but do not attach the resistor yet. Note that each capacitor is

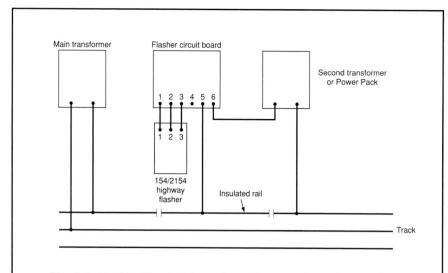

Fig. 3-7. Flasher Circuit Using a Second Transformer or Power Pack

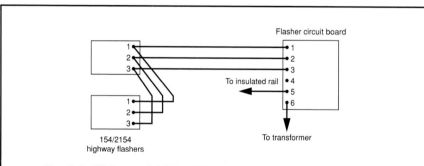

Fig. 3-8. Wiring an Additional Flasher for Simultaneous Operation

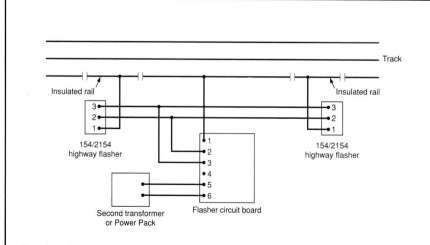

Fig. 3-9. Flasher Circuit Wired for Independent Operation of Two Flashers

connected to the base of one transistor and the collector of the other. Note too that each positive capacitor lead goes to a collector, and each negative capacitor lead to a base.

❑ Stop and check your work.

At this point, except for the resistors, the circuit is completely wired. Check to see that all the connections and polarities are correct and also that neighboring solder joints do not touch each other. If the joints or leads are too close together, use the small screwdriver to push them apart. Make sure that no stray wires touch the heatsink, since it is normally electrically connected to the negative (middle) terminal of the voltage regulator.

❑ Referring to fig. 3-2, cut the resistor leads to size, and coil the ends with the paper clip.

❑ Solder one lead of each resistor to the wire coming from the output (right-hand) terminal of the voltage regulator.

❑ Solder the other lead of resistor R1 to the wire coming from the negative lead of capacitor C2.

❑ Solder the other lead of the resistor R2 to the wire coming from the negative lead of capacitor C1

❑ Test the circuit. Connect the AC terminals of the barrier strip (5 and 6) to a 12- to 20-volt source, and the three output terminals (1, 2, and 3) to a highway flasher. Terminal 1 of the barrier strip is the common connection, and it goes to the rear (no. 1) post of the Lionel 154 flasher or to the center post of the Marx flasher. Now connect terminals 2 and 3 of the barrier strip to the remaining binding posts on the flasher—the order does not matter. The bulbs should go on and off alternately about 100 times a minute. If they flicker instead of flashing alternately, try a higher voltage.

If you are still not satisfied with the flashing rate of the circuit, you can change it by replacing the two timing resistors, R1 and R2. Larger resistors slow the flashes down, while smaller resistors speed them up. To slow the flashes down, try 4.7-kilohm resistors; to speed them up, try 3.3-kilohm units. To remove the old resistors, heat the joints with the soldering pencil and pull the resistors off. If that doesn't work, use a desoldering braid and a soldering gun.

INSTALL THE CIRCUIT ON THE LAYOUT

Operation from track voltage. In the simplest installation, the circuit operates directly from track voltage (see figs. 3-4 and 3-5). Two wires supply power, one connected to the third rail, and one to a 145C contactor or an insulated running rail. The 145C contactor also requires a separate connection to the ground.

The 145C contactor is a pressure operated off-on switch with two terminals. If you use it, you will need three additional wires: one from terminal 5 of the barrier strip to the third rail; a second from one contactor terminal to the running rail; and a third from the remaining contactor terminal to terminal 6 of the barrier strip. You can use an ordinary lockon for the two connections to the track.

The insulated running rail requires more work to install but is much more reliable. To insulate a running rail, insert plastic pins in each end and cardboard strips between the rail and the metal ties. The cardboard from a matchbook or cereal box works well. Make sure that the rail does not touch the ties anywhere. (For more information, see Peter Riddle's detailed discussion on making tracks with insulated running rails in his *Greenberg's Wiring Your Lionel Layout, Vol. II: Intermediate Techniques.*) You can also purchase track with insulated running rails.

Operation from fixed voltage. At very low track voltages, the lights

might flicker instead of flashing properly. To cure this problem, you can power the circuit from the fixed-voltage post of your transformer, if it has one, as shown in fig. 3-6. Make sure that the fixed-voltage post supplies at least 12 volts. In this circuit, one wire goes from the fixed voltage post on the transformer to terminal 6 on the barrier strip, and the other from a connection with the insulated running rail to terminal 5 on the strip.

Operation from an independent power supply. If your transformer does not have a fixed-voltage post, you can use an independent power supply, either a second transformer or an HO power pack (see fig. 3-7). The circuit will work as well on DC as on AC. Because of its low output, however, an HO power pack should be used to supply no more than two flashers. To power three or four flashers, use a small O27 starter transformer. In either case, connect one terminal of the power source to a ground such as an uninsulated running rail, and the other to terminal 6 on the circuit. Connect terminal 5 to the insulated rail, as above.

Simultaneous operation of additional flashers. The circuit shown in fig. 3-8 can power up to four flashers, either simultaneously or independently. To operate up to four highway flashers simultaneously, wire the additional flashers in parallel with the first one. To keep the voltage regulator from getting too hot, use low current no. 52 (screw-base) or no. 53 (bayonet) bulbs. These bulbs use about .1 amp at 12 volts. For a single flasher, the less efficient (.15-amp) no. 1445 or no. 1447 bulbs will do. If red bulbs are not available, you can spray-paint clear ones with aerosol enamel from an auto parts store.

Independent operation of additional flashers. For independent operation of more than one highway flasher, a separate power

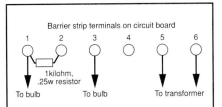

Fig. 3-10. The Circuit Wired as a Blinker; Barrier Strip Layout

supply is necessary. See fig. 3-9. Connect the power source directly to terminals 5 and 6 of the barrier strip. Then connect terminal 1 to a ground, such as an uninsulated running rail. Next, connect the common terminal of each flasher (terminal 1 on Lionel flashers and the center terminal on Marx units) to the adjacent insulated rail. Finally, connect terminals 2 and 3 on the strip to their respective terminals on each flasher. Each highway flasher will operate only when the train passes over the insulated rail adjacent to it.

Using the circuit as a blinker. You can wire this circuit as a blinker. This is especially useful for older blinking accessories whose thermostatic blinker strips no longer work. These include the prewar 79 traffic and crossing signal ("Diver's Helmet") and the 87 railroad crossing signal ("Bull's Eye"), as well as the postwar 193 flashing tower and the 410 billboard blinker.

To wire the circuit as a blinker, connect a 1-kilohm, .25-watt resistor between terminals 1 and 2. Connect the bulb leads to terminals 1 and 3. Bypass the thermostatic strip, if any. Use a no. 52 or no. 53 bulb (see figs. 3-10 and 3-11). As a blinker, the circuit can power up to four lights connected in parallel.

Using the circuit as a bell ringer for the 069 warning signal. The operating mechanism of the 069 warning signal is identical to that of a doorbell. It consists of an electromagnet and a spring-loaded

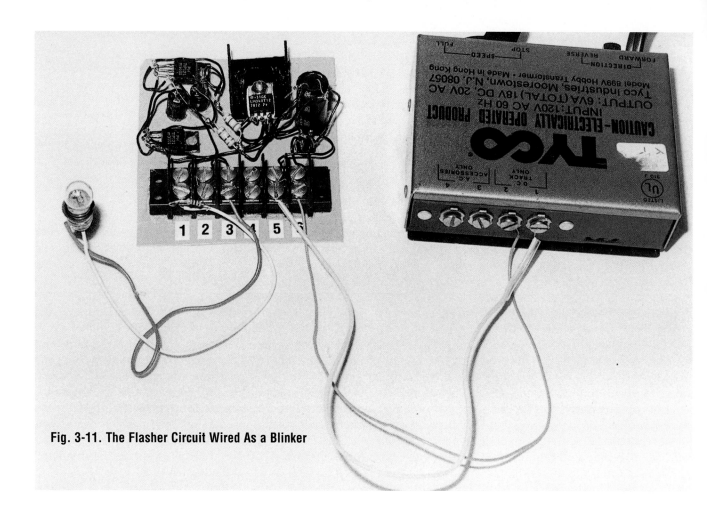

Fig. 3-11. The Flasher Circuit Wired As a Blinker

bar, or armature, which opens and closes a set of contacts. Together, the armature and contact assembly are known as the interrupter. Attached to the interrupter is a hammer that strikes either of two gongs. When the device is turned on, the electromagnet pulls the armature, ringing the bell and simultaneously opening the contacts. Opening the contacts shuts off the electromagnet, releasing the armature, which springs back to its original position. The contacts then close, energizing the electromagnet and ringing the bell again.

This cycle is repeated several times a second, so that the 069 signal not only works like a doorbell, but sounds like one. With the flasher circuit, however, and a few modifications, you can make it ring more prototypically. You will need two 10-ohm, 10-watt power resistors (271-132) or a single 20-ohm, 10-watt resistor (Digi-Key 20W-10-ND), three 1-kilohm, .25-watt resistors (271-1321), and a 1N4003 diode (276-1102).

The procedure is as follows (refer to figs. 3-12 and 3-13):

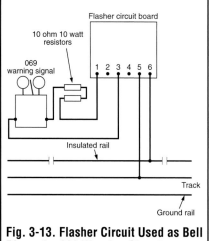

Fig. 3-12. Flasher Circuit Used as Bell Ringer; Barrier Strip Layout

Fig. 3-13. Flasher Circuit Used as Bell Ringer for 069 Warning Signal

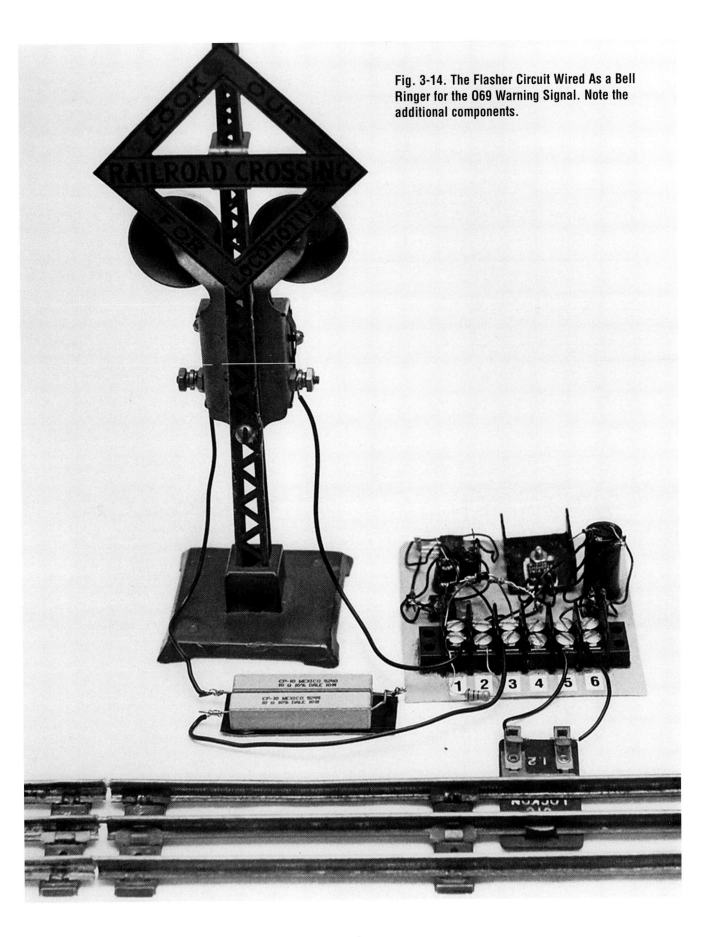

Fig. 3-14. The Flasher Circuit Wired As a Bell Ringer for the O69 Warning Signal. Note the additional components.

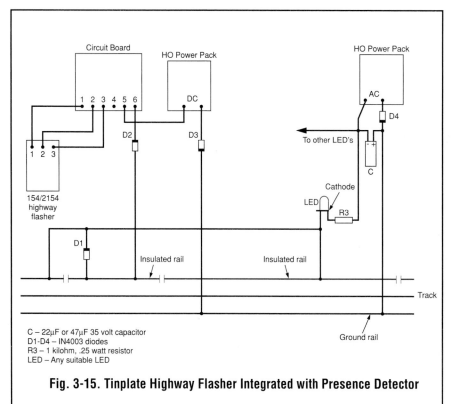

C – 22μF or 47μF 35 volt capacitor
D1-D4 – IN4003 diodes
R3 – 1 kilohm, .25 watt resistor
LED – Any suitable LED

Fig. 3-15. Tinplate Highway Flasher Integrated with Presence Detector

❑ Bypass the interrupter contacts; otherwise, the signal will continue to sound like a doorbell. To do this, you must remove the fiber washer that insulates one terminal of the electromagnet from the ground. Hold the signal upright so that the gongs face you and the warning sign points away from you. Remove the binding post nut and the locknut from the left binding post. Then, with a small screwdriver, pry off the large fiber insulating washer under the locknut on the metal surface. Do not remove the small fiber washer in the hole underneath. Finally, replace the locknut and the binding post nut.

❑ Replace the two 3.9-kilohm timing resistors on the circuit board with two 1-kilohm units. They will ring the signal at a more prototypical rate.

❑ Connect the third 1-kilohm resistor between terminals 1 and 2 of the barrier strip.

❑ Connect the diode between terminals 1 and 3, cathode (banded end) towards terminal 1. This diode protects the transistor from back emf generated by the electromagnet.

❑ Connect the warning signal to the 10-watt power resistors and to the circuit board. The power resistors protect the electromagnet from burning out. A single 20-ohm, 10-watt unit will also work. Connect a wire from one binding post on the signal to terminal 1 of the barrier strip. Then, referring to fig. 3-14, connect the 10-ohm resistors in series between the other binding post and terminal 3 of the barrier strip.

❑ Now test the circuit by connecting terminals 5 and 6 of the barrier strip to a 12- to 20-volt AC source. You will probably not get a good ring, since the gongs and

hammer are most likely out of tune.

❑ Adjust the hammer and gongs. While the signal is ringing, adjust the hammer to insure that it strikes only one gong and yields a good clear ring. Locate the adjustment screw on the left side of the case where it passes through a metal tab. Then turn it slowly and carefully. You may also have to rotate one or both gongs. When you get a good sound, tighten the screws securing the gongs.

❑ Quiet the armature if necessary. If the clicking of the armature and electromagnet is too obtrusive, you can muffle it somewhat with a piece of electrical tape on the end of the electromagnet, facing the armature. To get to the electromagnet and armature, pull the metal cover off the mechanism, taking care to guide the bell hammer through its slot.

❑ Install the warning signal and circuit board on the layout. Like the highway flasher, this circuit can also be powered by fixed voltage or a separate transformer. Because of heavy current consumption, a single power pack and circuit board can supply no more than one warning signal. The power resistors may run warm, but that is normal.

Integrating the highway flasher and presence detector. Like the stop circuit, the highway flasher can be integrated with the presence detector. As fig. 3-15 shows, the wiring is similar. Note that the same precautions must be observed: the stop circuit must be powered from the DC terminals of its own separate power pack, and the diodes must be installed exactly as indicated. When integrated, neither circuit may use track voltage or fixed voltage from the same transformer that powers the track. If the highway flasher doesn't work at first, flip the reversing switch on the power pack.

AN AUTOMATIC SWITCH FOR TWO-COLOR SIGNALS

PARTS, MATERIALS, AND TOOLS
Electronic parts
(Asterisks denote timing components, which differ from those of the highway flasher.)

Bridge rectifier, 100-volt, 1.4-amp (276-1152)

One 470-µF, 25- or 35-volt radial-lead electrolytic capacitor (272-1030).

*Two 2200-µF, 25- or 35-volt axial-lead electrolytic capacitors (272-1020) These replace 220-µF capacitors in the highway flasher. For longer intervals, use 4700-µF capacitors (272-1022).

*Two 3.3-K, .25-watt or .5-watt resistors (271-1328 or 271-1122). These and the 47-K pots replace the 3.9-K timing resistors.

*Two 47-K, .1-watt trimmer pots (271-283)

Two TIP 120 NPN Darlington, power transistors (276-2068)

One 7812 voltage regulator (276-1771)

Other parts, materials, and tools are identical to those used in the highway flasher.

The following circuit can liven up the 153 block signal and other two-color signals. This circuit (fig. 3-16) alternately turns each signal light on and off at a rate set by adjusting two components with a screwdriver. While not exactly prototypical, the circuit does not require modifying the track or using the fussy 153C contractor. It is easy to construct and

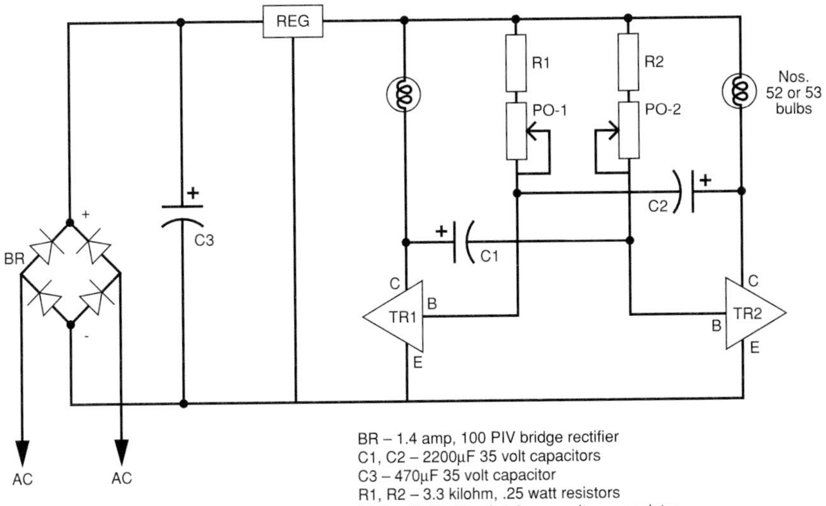

BR – 1.4 amp, 100 PIV bridge rectifier
C1, C2 – 2200µF 35 volt capacitors
C3 – 470µF 35 volt capacitor
R1, R2 – 3.3 kilohm, .25 watt resistors
REG – 7812, 12 volt 1.0 amp voltage regulator
TR1, TR2 – TIP 120 NPN Darlington power transistors
PO-1, PO-2 – 47 kilohm, 0.1 watt trimmer pots

Fig. 3-16. Circuit Schematic—Automatic Signal Switch

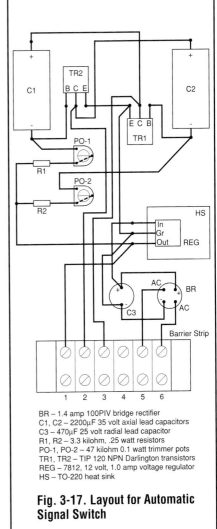

BR – 1.4 amp 100PIV bridge rectifier
C1, C2 – 2200µF 35 volt axial lead capacitors
C3 – 470µF 25 volt radial lead capacitor
R1, R2 – 3.3 kilohm, .25 watt resistors
PO-1, PO-2 – 47 kilohm 0.1 watt trimmer pots
TR1, TR2 – TIP 120 NPN Darlington transistors
REG – 7812, 12 volt, 1.0 amp voltage regulator
HS – TO-220 heat sink

Fig. 3-17. Layout for Automatic Signal Switch

Fig. 3-18. The Completed Automatic Signal Switch

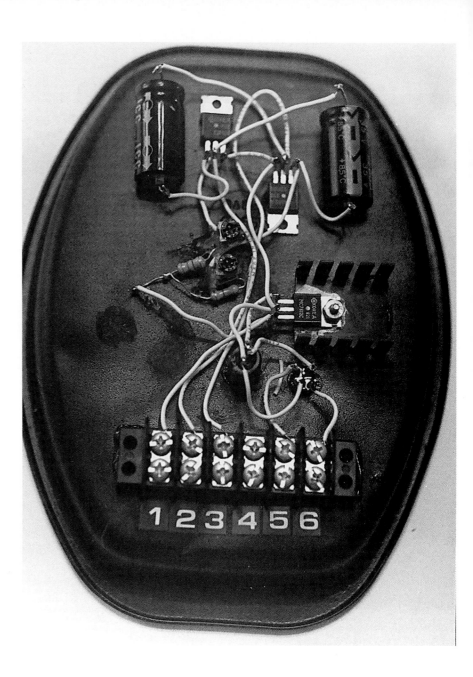

install, and should not require further attention once in place. Except for the timing components, this circuit is constructed much like the highway flasher circuit.

OPERATION

This circuit operates like the highway flasher. The period during which each light is turned on can be adjusted from a few seconds to approximately one minute. With 4700-microfarad capacitors instead of the specified 2200-microfarad units, the period can be increased to two minutes per light.

PREPARE THE PARTS, MOUNT THEM, AND WIRE THE CIRCUIT

Because the timing capacitors and trimmer pots take up more room, the layout (figs. 3-17 and 3-18) differs from that of the highway flasher. Besides being larger, the timing capacitors have axial leads (leads sticking out of each end), which make mounting and wiring somewhat awkward. Otherwise, the wiring is the same, except that a 47-kilohm trimmer pot and 3.3-kilohm resistor replace each 3.9-kilohm timing resistor.

To build this circuit, follow the instructions for constructing the highway flasher through "Stop and check your work" in the section headed "Wire the circuit," earlier in this chapter. Take the differences in layout into account, referring to fig. 3-17. Stop after you have checked everything.

Next, turn to Chapter 2 and follow

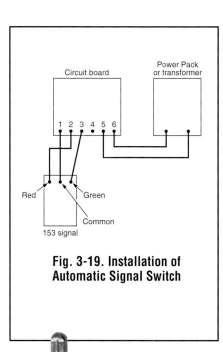

Fig. 3-19. Installation of Automatic Signal Switch

instructions for constructing the trimmer pot and resistor assembly. Make two of these assemblies. Now join them together and install them in the circuit as follows:

❏ Use the straightened paper clip to make a loop consisting of two or three closely spaced turns in the remaining lead of one resistor.

❏ Slide this loop onto the lead of the second resistor.

❏ With needle-nose pliers, squeeze the loop tight ¼" from the second resistor, and solder it.

❏ Attach the two trimmer pots to the microwave dinner tray with silicone sealant and let it cure overnight. Do not get sealant inside these devices or on the adjustment screws.

❏ Solder the lead you connected ¼" from the second resistor to the wire coming from the output (right-hand) terminal of the voltage regulator.

❏ Solder the wire from one pot (PO1) to the wire coming from the negative terminal of capacitor C1. The connections in this step and the following one differ slightly from those in fig. 2-3. This should not make any difference in operation.

❏ Solder the wire from the other pot (PO2) to the wire coming from the negative terminal of capacitor C2.

INSTALL AND ADJUST THE CIRCUIT

Refer to figs. 3-19 and 3-20. The wires from the transformer or

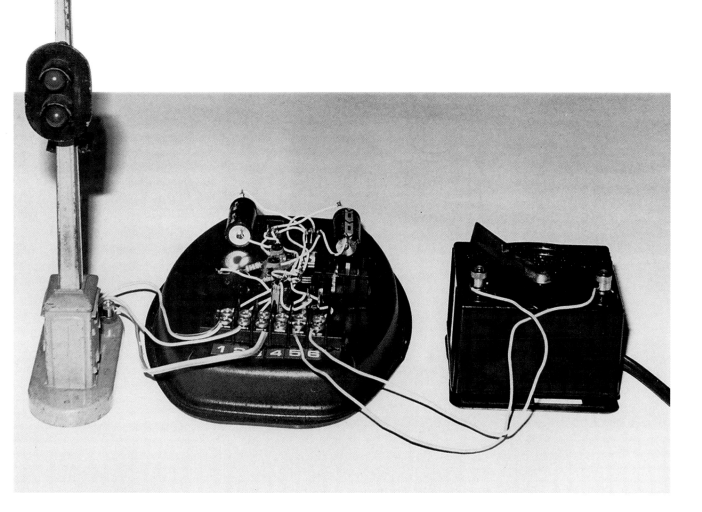

Fig. 3-20. Testing the Automatic Signal Switch

power pack go to terminals 5 and 6 of the barrier strip. The wire from the common (center) binding post of the signal goes to terminal 1, while the wires from the other two binding posts go to terminals 2 and 3, respectively.

To test the circuit, first turn the adjustment screw on each pot counterclockwise as far as it will go. Turn the current on. Each light should flash alternately every second or few seconds. Turn the current off. Now move each adjustment screw clockwise about a quarter turn and repeat the test. The period during which each light is on should increase. Keep turning the adjustment screw until you are satisfied. The maximum is approximately one minute for each light. As noted above, 4700-micro-farad capacitors can increase the maximum time to about two minutes per light.

A high degree of precision is not possible with this circuit, as the timing capacitors have loose tolerance, generally in the order of plus or minus 20 percent. As a result, with similar settings on the pots, the lights might be turned on for somewhat different lengths of time.

4

Circuit for Bachmann/Plasticville Highway Flashers

Lionel and Marx highway flashers are massively oversized. If you prefer something closer to scale, why not modify a Bachmann/Plasticville warning signal? These are sold in sets of six, together with plastic crossing gates. Unfortunately, they are unpowered, with only red plastic inserts where flashing lights should be. You can remedy this situation, however, with two LEDs and a circuit similar to that described in Chapter 3.

HOW THE CIRCUIT WORKS

Because this circuit consumes less current than the preceding one, it can use lighter components. In other respects it is similar, as a comparison of figs. 3-1 and 4-1 shows.

The small signal or power diode serves the same purpose as a bridge rectifier, converting AC to DC. It works by passing current in only one direction. This cuts off about half the current, but that doesn't matter much, since very little current (10 to 50 milliamps) is needed for operation. Less current means also that a smaller (100-microfarad) filter capacitor can be used and that small general-purpose transistors can replace the Darlington power units of the preceding circuit.

The 150-ohm resistor drops the voltage slightly, while the 1-kilohm resistors limit current to the LEDs. The 47-kilohm resistors and 22-microfarad capacitors form the timing portion of the circuit.

The two LEDs are specially designed to emit red light when a current is passed through them. The LEDs in this circuit use a tenth as much current as the light bulbs in the previous one. Unlike light bulbs, however, LEDs are polarized and must be connected properly. In addition, they need current limiting resistors.

Because the circuit uses little current and functions well on an AC input of 12 to 16 volts, it does not need a large voltage regulator and heatsink. You can also use the 20-volt AC terminals of an HO

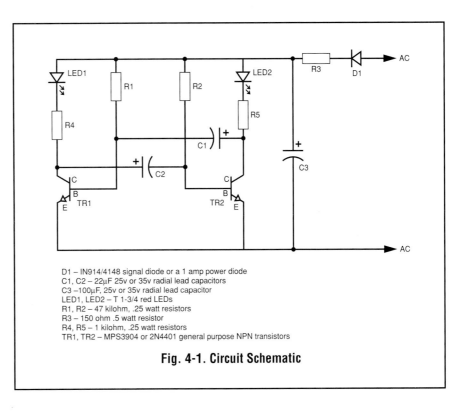

D1 – IN914/4148 signal diode or a 1 amp power diode
C1, C2 – 22µF 25v or 35v radial lead capacitors
C3 –100µF, 25v or 35v radial lead capacitor
LED1, LED2 – T 1-3/4 red LEDs
R1, R2 – 47 kilohm, .25 watt resistors
R3 – 150 ohm .5 watt resistor
R4, R5 – 1 kilohm, .25 watt resistors
TR1, TR2 – MPS3904 or 2N4401 general purpose NPN transistors

Fig. 4-1. Circuit Schematic

PARTS, MATERIALS, AND TOOLS

Parts needed to modify warning signal

Bachmann/Plasticville highway warning signal

Two 1-K, .25-watt resistors (271-1321)

Two red T-1 3/4 LEDs (276-041)

White 30 gauge kynar wrapping wire (278-502)

Two 330-ohm, .5-watt resistors (271-1113). For operators who choose to modify the tinplate flasher circuit rather than construct the circuit described in this chapter. See the text.

Other parts for circuit board

One IN914/4148 small signal diode (276-1122 or 276-1620). A 1-amp power diode (276-1101) will also work.

Two 22-µF, 25- or 35-volt radial-lead capacitors (272-1026)

100-µF, 25- or 35-volt radial-lead capacitor (272-1028)

One or two 150-ohm, .5-watt resistors (271-1109). If you plan to power the circuit from the 20-volt AC terminals of an HO power pack, use a single 390-ohm, .5-watt resistor (271-1114).

Two 47-K, .25-watt resistors (271-1342)

Two MPS3904 or 2N4401 general-purpose NPN transistors (276-2016, 276-2058). Any general-purpose NPN transistor with a collector current rating (I_c) of 100 milliamps or more will work.

One six-position barrier strip (274-659)

Additional parts and materials

22 or 24 gauge wire

Silicone rubber sealant (64-2314)

.032 rosin-core solder (64-005). Do not use acid-core solder; it will corrode the joints.

IC spacing perfboard (276-1395, 276-1394, or 276-1396)

Plastic microwave dinner tray large enough to yield a square about 3" on each side

Medium-grade sandpaper

Damp sponge

Numbers from a videotape label

CA adhesive (Superglue, Crazy Glue)

Correction fluid (White Out, Over-All, etc.)

Masking tape

Toothpick

Tools

Wire-wrapping tool (276-1570)

15-watt soldering pencil (64-2051)

Medium-size screwdriver

Small (1/8") slotted screwdriver

Needle-nose pliers (64-1812 or 64-1844)

Wire stripper/cutter (64-1952 or 64-2129)

Helping Hands (64-2093)

One sixpenny nail

Hair dryer

Drill and 1/16" bit

---

power pack provided you replace the 150-ohm voltage-dropping resistor with a 390-ohm, .5-watt unit. Or you can connect an additional 220-ohm resistor between the power pack and the circuit board.

PREPARE THE HIGHWAY SIGNAL

Unlike the tinplate flashers, which are wired and ready to install, the Plasticville/Bachmann unit must be modified for operation. The first task is to ream out the holes in which the LEDs will be mounted. With the utility knife, cut three or four squares of medium-grade (no. 80) sandpaper approximately 3/4" x 1". Wrap one of them tightly around the sixpenny nail, and insert it in one of the holes in the flasher, as fig. 4-2

shows. Rotate the nail and sandpaper several times to remove some of the plastic. Then pull the nail and sandpaper out and, from the back of the flasher, try to insert an LED. If the LED goes in easily all the way, do the other hole. If not, ream out the first hole some more. The back of each LED should be flush with the back of the flasher. Don't try to force the LEDs or you will damage them and possibly the flasher.

After you have reamed out the holes, drill a 1/16" hole in the base, right behind the post for the wires from the LEDs. If you plan to cover the base with scenery, you can dispense with the hole and simply run the wires over the base.

Take the LEDs out and reinsert

them in their holes, so that the cathode (shorter lead) of each LED is on the outside. You can also identify the cathode by a flat or notched area near it on the edge of the case. The remaining two leads (on the inside, facing each other) are the anodes or positive terminals (fig. 4-3). If an LED is too loose and seems likely to fall out, a drop of CA adhesive applied from the back will hold it in place. Trim the leads to about 1/2".

For the next step, use the wire-wrapping tool and its enclosed stripper. If you have never used these tools before, you might want to practice first with a wrapping post from an IC socket or an LED. Pull off the end of the wire-wrapping tool and remove the wire stripper. Cut about 6" of wrapping wire and insert the wire in the slotted blade of the wire stripper so that about ½" protrudes from the side with the screw. Bend this piece down, and pull the wire from behind. The insulation should come right off. Strip the other end in the same way.

Next insert the stripped piece of wire in the end of the wire-wrapping tool, making sure it goes into the opening near the edge and not into the center hole. The wire will emerge along the side. Clamp the signal in the Helping Hands so that the leads of the LED face up. Bend the unstripped section of wire at right angles to the end of the tool, insert the cathode (shorter) lead of the LED into the center hole of the wire-wrapping tool, and push the tool all the way down. Holding the wire with one hand, turn the tool clockwise several tines until the wire is completely wrapped around the cathode. Remove the tool.

Cut another 6" of wire and attach it to the other cathode. Then run both wires through the hole in the base. Trim the cathode leads of the LEDs down to the wrapping wire joints.

Now slide a ¾" length of ¹⁄₁₆" heat-shrink tubing onto each wire. Cut the leads of each 1-kilohm resistor down to about ½", and solder one wire to each resistor. Slide the heat-shrink tubing over the joint, and holding a hot hair dryer close to the joint, shrink the tubing in place. Finally, solder a 6" piece of 22 or 24 gauge wire to the other end of each resistor. Then slide a length of heat-shrink tubing over the joint, and shrink it in place (see fig. 4-4).

Attach a third 6" length of wrapping wire to one anode, but do not trim the lead yet. Run this wire through the hole in the base (or over the base). Next, run a wire from this anode to the other. If you accidentally strip all the insu-

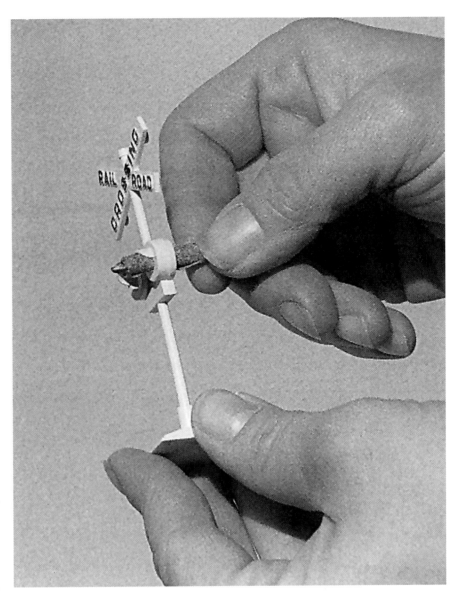

Fig. 4-2. Reaming the Flasher

lation off, don't worry. Just make sure the bare wire doesn't touch either of the cathode connections. When you have finished these connections, you can trim the anode leads. Because the LED leads are square, their joints do not require soldering, and in any event will later be sealed with correction fluid.

The next step is to camouflage the wiring. Smooth the three wires out, and run them along the back of the post, parallel and close

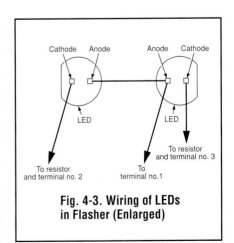

Fig. 4-3. Wiring of LEDs in Flasher (Enlarged)

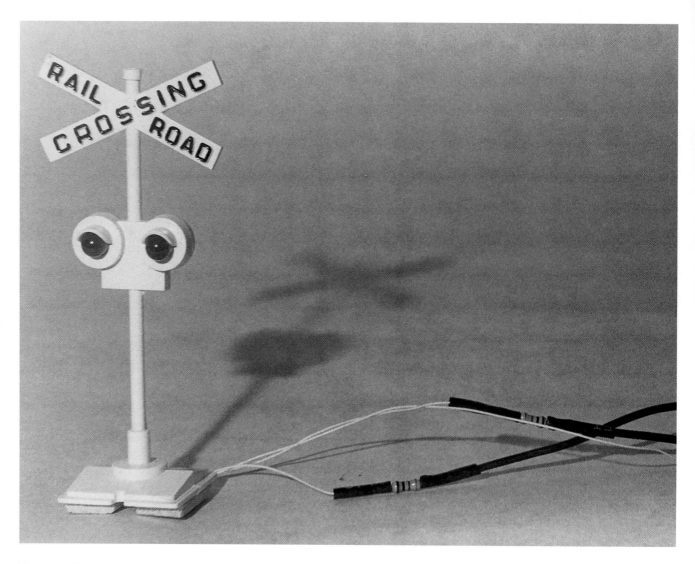

Fig. 4-4. Flasher with Wires and Resistors Attached

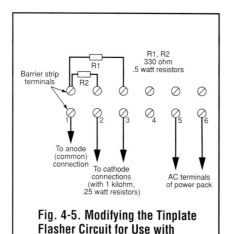

Fig. 4-5. Modifying the Tinplate Flasher Circuit for Use with Bachmann/Plasticville Flashers

together. You can use small pieces of masking tape at top and bottom to hold the wires tight against the post. With a toothpick, apply CA adhesive to the wires along the post. When the joint has dried (in 15 to 30 seconds), remove the pieces of masking tape and apply adhesive to the remaining sections of the wires lying against the post. After everything is dry, brush correction fluid onto the backs of the LEDs, the sections of bare wire, the wrapping wire connections, and the wires along the post. Allow the correction fluid a few minutes to dry, and then apply a second

coat to the backs of the LEDs. If light shows through later, when the flasher is working, apply a third coat.

Glue two thin pieces of wood (craft sticks will do) under the base, as shown in fig. 4-4, in order to raise the flasher and provide a path for the wires.

Regarding the circuit itself, you have two options. You can construct the circuit described in the next section, which is specially designed for LED flashers, or you can modify the tinplate flasher circuit described in Chapter 3. To modify the tinplate flasher circuit,

Fig. 4-6. Tinplate Flasher Modified for Use with LEDs

connect one 330-ohm, .5-watt resistor between terminal 1 and terminal 2, and an identical resistor between terminal 1 and terminal 3 (see figs. 4-5 and 4-6).

The modified circuit does not flash quite as cleanly as the specially designed circuit. But it should still be acceptable for most operators. When you connect the highway signal to the modified tinplate circuit, the common (anode) lead goes to terminal 1, while each cathode lead (with the 1-kilohm resistor) goes to terminal 2 and 3, respectively.

PREPARE AND MOUNT THE PARTS

Mount the electronic components on a piece of perfboard approximately 1" x 1⅜". To cut a piece that size, first score the perf-board with a utility knife, and then break it along the scored lines.

Before you proceed, take a moment to examine one of the transistors. Like the larger Darlingtons in the preceding chapter, this transistor has three terminals: a base, a collector, and an emitter. Their order, however, is different: with the flat side of the case down, and the pins pointing towards you, the collector is on the left, the base is in the center, and the emitter is on the right.

Bend the leads of the transistors so that they will fit easily in the perfboard holes, flat side down, as shown in fig. 4-7. First, bend them with pliers at right angles about 1/16" from the case, toward the flat side. Then bend the two end leads up and out, so that they each point in opposite directions.

Fig. 4-7. Bending the Transistor Leads before Mounting

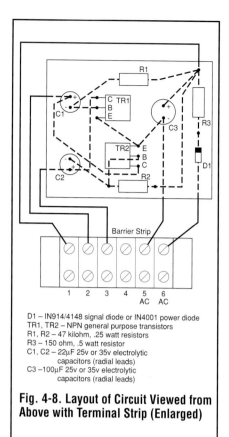

D1 – IN914/4148 signal diode or IN4001 power diode
TR1, TR2 – NPN general purpose transistors
R1, R2 – 47 kilohm, .25 watt resistors
R3 – 150 ohm, .5 watt resistor
C1, C2 – 22μF 25v or 35v electrolytic
    capacitors (radial leads)
C3 –100μF 25v or 35v electrolytic
    capacitors (radial leads)

Fig. 4-8. Layout of Circuit Viewed from Above with Terminal Strip (Enlarged)

Finally, bend the end leads down, but just far enough from the center (base) lead that the transistors will fit nicely into the holes on the perfboard.

The last parts to be prepared for mounting are the diode and resistors. Bend their leads at right angles, parallel to each other, about 1/16" from the case, so that they will fit into the perfboard holes.

Insert the parts in the perfboard, following the layout in figs. 4-8 and 4-9. Make sure the transistors and capacitors and diode are aligned properly. Insert transistor TR1, flat side down, with its leads pointing left, no more than 1/4" from capacitor C1. Then insert transistor TR2 flat side down, with its leads pointing right. The emitters of each transistor will then face each other on the inside, and the collectors will be on the outside. Make sure also that the negative leads of capacitors C1 and C2 face each other and that the positive lead of

capacitor C3 faces the top edge of the perfboard, so that this capacitor is above and to the left of the diode. Finally, make sure that the cathode (banded end) of the diode faces resistor R3. Check everything and, when you are satisfied with the layout, secure the parts in place with silicone sealant. This will make wiring the circuit, which must be done from the underside, much easier. Allow the sealant to cure overnight.

WIRE THE CIRCUIT

Before you start wiring the circuit, orient yourself by examining figs. 4-8 and 4-9. Hold the circuit board upside down, and turn it until the diode is in the upper right corner. Bend the anode lead (from the unbanded end of the diode), so that it faces out and away from you, as shown in fig. 4-10. This will go to terminal 6 of the barrier strip. Now join the cathode lead (from the banded end of the diode)

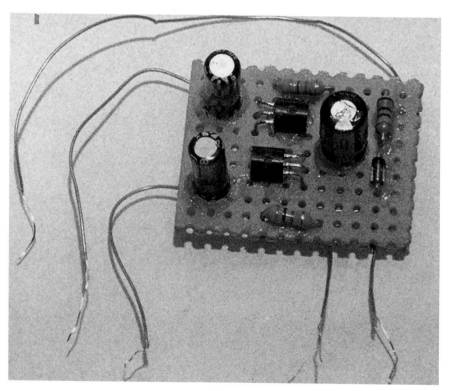

Fig. 4-9. The Circuit Mounted on Perfboard, Viewed from Above

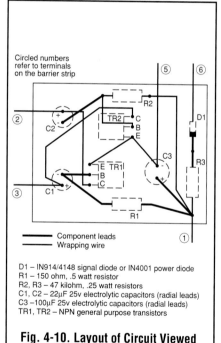

Circled numbers refer to terminals on the barrier strip

━━━ Component leads
——— Wrapping wire

D1 – IN914/4148 signal diode or IN4001 power diode
R1 – 150 ohm, .5 watt resistor
R2, R3 – 47 kilohm, .25 watt resistors
C1, C2 – 22μF 25v electrolytic capacitors (radial leads)
C3 –100μF 25v electrolytic capacitors (radial leads)
TR1, TR2 – NPN general purpose transistors

Fig. 4-10. Layout of Circuit Viewed From Underneath (Enlarged)

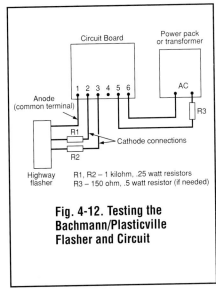

Fig. 4-12. Testing the Bachmann/Plasticville Flasher and Circuit

R1, R2 – 1 kilohm, .25 watt resistors
R3 – 150 ohm, .5 watt resistor (if needed)

Circuit Board

Power pack or transformer

Anode (common terminal)

Cathode connections

Highway flasher

Fig. 4-11. The Completed Circuit Board

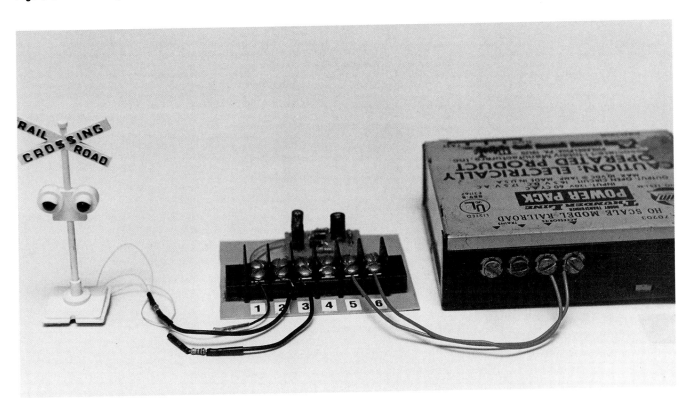

Fig. 4-13. Testing the Flasher and Its Circuit

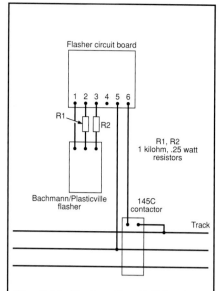

Fig. 4-14. Flasher Circuit Using Track Voltage and 145C Contactor

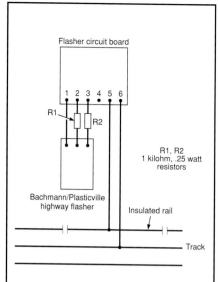

Fig. 4-15. Flasher Circuit Using Track Voltage and Insulated Rail

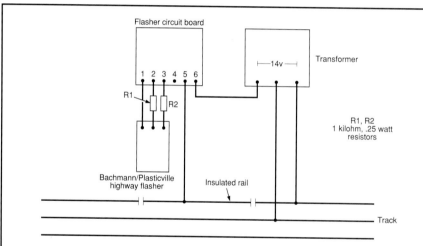

Fig. 4-16. Flasher Circuit Using a Single Transformer and Fixed Voltage

to resistor R3. Simply twist the leads together close to the perfboard, and cut off the excess.

The other lead to resistor R3 is the positive DC terminal and goes to the most complicated junction in the circuit. Find the positive lead to capacitor C3, and join it to the R3 lead. With the needle-nose pliers, wind one lead around the other once or twice and squeeze the joint until it is good and tight. Use the

wire strippers to trim the twisted lead down to the joint. Next join the lead from resistor R1 to this junction in the same way, except that when you trim the lead down, leave a piece about ⅜". This is for a connection to resistor R2, which you will make later. Finally, bend the long (untrimmed) lead down and out, so that it faces toward you. This lead is the common connection and will go to terminal 1.

Turn to transistor TR1 and find the base, which is the middle lead. Use the needle-nose pliers to wrap the base lead around the negative lead of capacitor C1. Then join the remaining lead from resistor R1 to the same capacitor lead, and trim off the excess. Leave a little slack, and make sure that this lead does not touch the collector (bottom) lead of transistor TR1. Finally, join the negative lead of capacitor C2 to the nearest lead of resistor R2, leaving a ⅜" piece when you trim it. At this point, cut all the remaining unconnected component leads to ½".

You will now need the wrapping wire and the wrapping tool to make the remaining connections. In fig. 4-10 thin lines represent wrapping wire, while thick lines represent connections made with component leads. Strip off no more insulation than you need for each joint, because the wire between the joints must remain insulated. As you complete each joint, cut the component lead down to the joint, except as noted.

Six connections on the circuit board are made with wrapping wire:
❑ From the emitter (inside lead) of transistor TR2 to the negative lead of capacitor C3. Do not cut this capacitor lead yet. It is for a connection to terminal 5 of the barrier strip. Do not cut this emitter lead until after you make the next connection.
❑ From the emitter (inside lead) of transistor TR2 to the emitter of transistor TR1.
❑ From resistor R1, at its junction with capacitor C3 and resistor R3, to resistor R2.
❑ From the junction of capacitor C2 and resistor R2 to the base (middle lead) of transistor TR2.
❑ From the collector (outside lead) of transistor TR1 to the positive lead of capacitor C2. Do not cut the capacitor lead yet. It is for a connection to terminal 2 of the barrier strip.

56

❑ From the collector (outside lead) of transistor TR2 to the positive lead of capacitor C1. Do not cut this capacitor lead yet either. It is for a connection to terminal 3 of the barrier strip.

At this point, stop and take a moment to check everything. Make sure that the polarities of the diode and the capacitors are correct, and that the transistors are oriented properly, emitters facing each other. Check that each timing capacitor (C1 and C2) is connected to the base of one transistor (or to a lead that goes to the base) and to the collector of the other. Make sure that each collector is connected to the positive lead of one timing capacitor, and that each base is connected to the negative lead of the other timing capacitor. Finally, make sure that no bare leads or joints touch each other.

Now you can solder the joints on the circuit board. The wrapping wire joints, especially, must be soldered, because the component leads are round and, without solder, the wrapping wire will work itself loose. Clamp the circuit board upside down in the Helping Hands. Whenever you solder a connection to a diode or transistor, clamp the soldering heat sink onto the lead, on the other side of the circuit board, between the joint and the case. Hold the hot soldering pencil against the joint and touch the solder to the joint. The solder should flow through it almost instantly. Remove the soldering pencil.

After you have finished soldering the joints on the circuit board, you can work on the wire connections to the barrier strip terminals, using wrapping wire or 22 to 24 gauge solid wire. Figures 4-8 and 4-11 will give you some idea of how long the wires should be and where they should go. There are five wire connections:

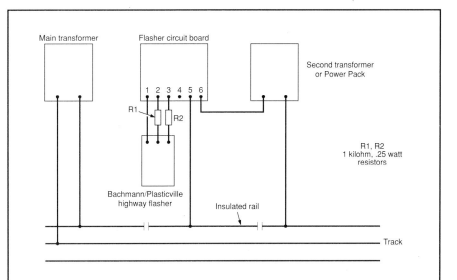

Fig. 4-17. Flasher Circuit Using a Second Transformer or Power Pack

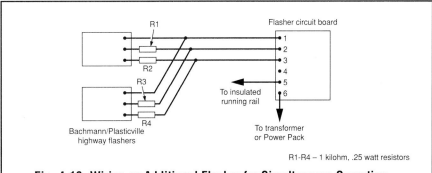

Fig. 4-18. Wiring an Additional Flasher for Simultaneous Operation

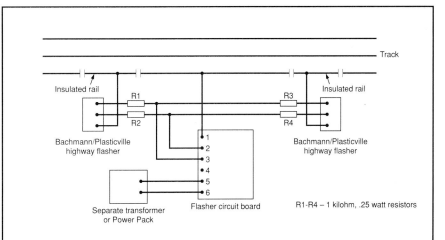

Fig. 4-19. Flasher Circuit Wired for Independent Operation of Two Flashers

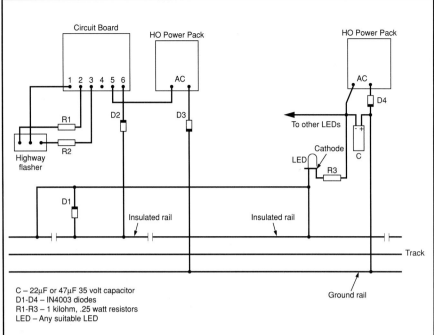

C – 22μF or 47μF 35 volt capacitor
D1-D4 – IN4003 diodes
R1-R3 – 1 kilohm, .25 watt resistors
LED – Any suitable LED

Fig. 4-20. Plasticville Highway Flasher Integrated with Presence Indicator

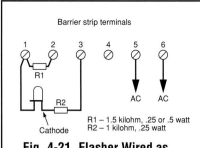

R1 – 1.5 kilohm, .25 or .5 watt
R2 – 1 kilohm, .25 watt

Fig. 4-21. Flasher Wired as a Blinker for a Single LED

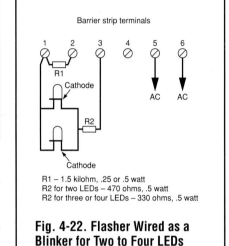

R1 – 1.5 kilohm, .25 or .5 watt
R2 for two LEDs – 470 ohms, .5 watt
R2 for three or four LEDs – 330 ohms, .5 watt

Fig. 4-22. Flasher Wired as a Blinker for Two to Four LEDs

❑ From resistor R3 at its junction with resistor R1 and capacitor C3 to terminal 1 of the barrier strip.
❑ From the positive lead of capacitor C1 to terminal 2.
❑ From the positive lead of capacitor C2 to terminal 3.
❑ From the negative lead of capacitor C3 to terminal 5.
❑ From the anode of the diode to terminal 6.

Measure the wires, cut them, and solder them to the appropriate leads. But do not attach them to their terminals in the barrier strip yet. As you complete each connection, cut off the excess component lead, so that it won't accidentally short against anything.

Attach the circuit board and the barrier strip to a piece of plastic from a microwave dinner tray with silicone sealant, and let it cure overnight. Label the terminals and remove the upper screw from each. Strip the end of each wire and wrap it around a screw. Then lower the

screw into its hole on the barrier strip and tighten it.

TEST AND INSTALL THE CIRCUIT

This circuit is tested and installed in much the same way as the tinplate flasher circuit (figs. 4-12 and 4-13). The barrier strip terminals of this circuit correspond to those of the tinplate highway flasher described in Chapter 3. The common (anode) lead of the flasher goes to terminal 1, while the cathode leads (wires with the 1-kilohm resistors) go to terminals 2 and 3, respectively. The 12- to 16-volt AC input goes to terminals 5 and 6. Consult figs. 4-14 through 4-19 for further details regarding connections to insulated rails, multiple signals, etc.

Like the tinplate flasher, this circuit can be integrated with the presence detector. The wiring is similar (fig. 4-20). In this arrangement, use the AC terminals of the two power packs. Make sure that

the diodes are connected properly.

With a few changes, this circuit can be wired as a blinker, either for a single LED or for up to four LEDs in unison. Using figs. 4-21 and 4-22 as a reference, connect a 1.5-kilohm, .25-watt unit between terminals 1 and 2. Make sure that the LED also has its own 1-kilohm current-limiting resistor. If you use the circuit as a blinker for two to four LEDs, you can use a single current-limiting resistor, as shown in fig. 4-22.

Note that the value of the current-limiting resistor (R2) depends on the number of LEDs. This resistor must be rated at no less than .5 watt.

5

Power Circuit for Tinplate switches

Balky at times and tending to burn out, tinplate switches are the source of much frustration. A simple electronic circuit, however, can greatly improve their performance and reliability. Originally developed for scale operation, this circuit is easily adapted to tinplate use. (The version presented below is modified from circuits previously published by Peter Thorne in his books *Practical Electronics for Model Railroaders* and *Model Railroad Electronics: Basic Concepts to Advanced Projects*.)

HOW TINPLATE SWITCHES WORK

Tinplate switches are powered by switch motors, each of which consists of two *solenoids*, hollow coils with a movable steel plunger inside. Each solenoid throws the switch by pulling the plunger in either of two directions. In order to throw the switch, each solenoid requires a brief pulse of heavy current, which it receives from the third rail or from a constant-voltage terminal on the transformer.

Switch motors are usually wired so that grounding a solenoid throws the switch, a design that makes the nonderailing feature possible. In switches equipped with this

feature, each solenoid is connected to an insulated running rail. A train approaching the switch grounds the insulated rail through its wheels, energizing the solenoid and throwing the switch in the proper direction.

The most common problems plaguing tinplate switches result from their current requirements. On the one hand, the third rail

may not provide enough current for them to operate at all. On the other hand, the heavy current these switches need in order to operate properly will burn them out if applied for more than a few seconds. This is a special problem for Lionel O27 switches equipped with the nonderailing feature. These switches lack special circuitry to disconnect the solenoids

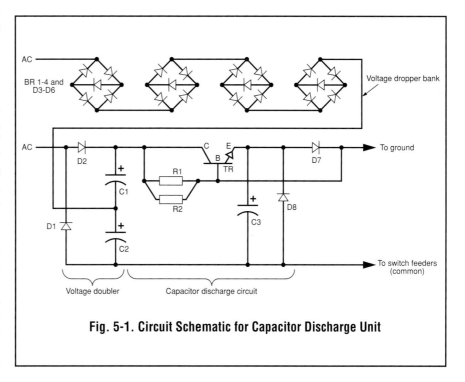

Fig. 5-1. Circuit Schematic for Capacitor Discharge Unit

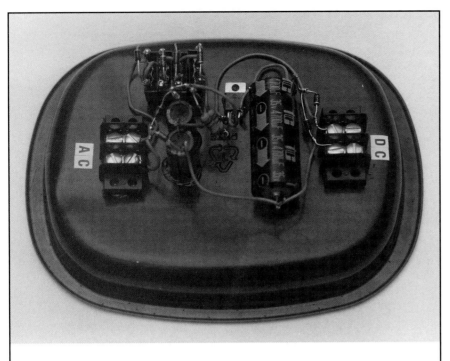

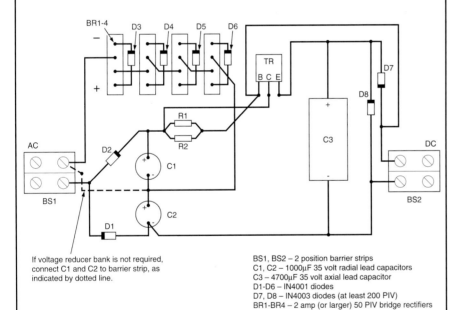

If voltage reducer bank is not required, connect C1 and C2 to barrier strip, as indicated by dotted line.

BS1, BS2 – 2 position barrier strips
C1, C2 – 1000µF 35 volt radial lead capacitors
C3 – 4700µF 35 volt axial lead capacitor
D1-D6 – IN4001 diodes
D7, D8 – IN4003 diodes (at least 200 PIV)
BR1-BR4 – 2 amp (or larger) 50 PIV bridge rectifiers
R1, R2 – 1 kilohm, 1 watt resistors
TR – TIP 3055 transistor

Fig. 5-2. Layout for Capacitor Discharge Unit

after operation. As a result, any rolling stock remaining on an insulated running rail will continue to energize the solenoid, overheating it. The circuit presented below will greatly improve the performance of the following switches: Lionel O27 switches, including MPC and LTI production; Marx switches; prewar Lionel 011 and 012 switches; and prewar American Flyer switches. Called a *capacitor discharge* (or *CD*) *unit,* the circuit provides enough energy for snappy operation of up to two switches at the same time. It eliminates the risk of burnout, and it is unaffected by changes in track voltage.

The circuit is of less value for Lionel 022 and K-Line switches. These switches use little current, can be powered from fixed voltage, and have circuitry designed to minimize the likelihood of burnout. Installing a CD unit necessitates doing without the indicator lights (or LEDs) on the controller or panel. For most operators with these switches, installing a CD unit is probably not worth the trouble. Nevertheless, instructions are provided for those who wish to do so.

HOW THE CIRCUIT WORKS

The circuit consists of three assemblies that work together as a single system (see figs. 5-1 and 5-2).

Voltage droppers. As shown in fig. 5-3, each voltage dropper consists of a bridge rectifier with a diode connected across its DC terminals, anode to positive lead. Each rectifier consists of a network of four diodes, only two of which are in operation at any one time. Because all silicon diodes have a constant voltage drop of about .6 volt, each rectifier and its external diode drop the voltage 1.8 volts. The polarity of the current does not affect the voltage droppers, and they can be installed on the AC side of the circuit.

The circuit uses up to four voltage

droppers to reduce the AC input voltage, to keep the DC output at approximately 35 volts. The number of voltage droppers required depends on the voltage of the AC power source.

Voltage doubler. The reduced AC voltage now goes to a voltage doubler, consisting of two 1000-microfarad capacitors and two diodes. The circuit charges the capacitors and adds their voltages together, more than doubling the AC voltage. Simultaneously, it converts the AC into DC, and filters it, so that a smooth current at higher voltage goes to the capacitor discharge circuit. However, because the total power must remain the same, the amperage is reduced proportionately.

Capacitor discharge circuit. The capacitor discharge circuit consists of two 1-kilohm, 1-watt resistors, a power transistor, a 4700-microfarad electrolytic capacitor, and two additional diodes that protect the unit from back emf originating in the solenoids.

Operation is as follows:

Stage 1: Capacitor charging; switch not thrown. Before the switch is thrown, about 70 milliamps flow through the resistor assembly into the base of the transistor, turning the transistor on. A much larger current flows through the collector and emitter of the transistor into the capacitor, charging it. In about two seconds, when the capacitor is fully charged, the flow of current stops.

Stage 2: Switch thrown; capacitor discharging. Throwing the switch closes the circuit, so that the capacitor discharges through a switch solenoid. For a few milliseconds, a very heavy current flows through the solenoid and back to the capacitor. Now energized, the solenoid pulls the plunger and shifts the switch points.

Stage 3: Capacitor discharged; circuit still closed. Normally, after

Fig. 5-3. A Diode and a Bridge Rectifier Wired As a Voltage Dropper

the capacitor discharges, the switch circuit opens, and the capacitor recharges, as in Stage 1. If, however, the switch contacts are stuck or if a car remains on the insulated running rail of a nonderailing switch, the switch circuit stays closed. Seventy milliamps now flow through the resistor assembly past the transistor and capacitor and on through the switch solenoid. The transistor remains turned off, and the capacitor does not charge. Current flows through the solenoid but is too weak to overheat it. The resistor assembly itself may get hot, but it should not burn out.

This circuit has two advantages. It allows a small AC source, such as the accessory terminals of an HO power pack, to provide the heavy current needed to operate the switch. And it protects the solenoid from burnout.

There is, however, a slight disadvantage: as long as one closed switch circuit prevents the capacitor from recharging, no other switch powered by the CD unit will work. For this reason, you might consider disconnecting the nonderailing feature from switches on which cars are likely to stand for long periods. Instructions for doing this are provided. You might

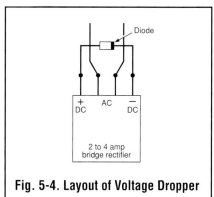

Fig. 5-4. Layout of Voltage Dropper

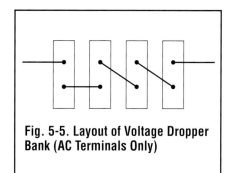

Fig. 5-5. Layout of Voltage Dropper Bank (AC Terminals Only)

also consider providing critical switches, such as those in reversing loops, with their own individual CD units. Once these adjustments are made, operation should be trouble free.

PREPARE AND MOUNT THE PARTS

Prepare the voltage droppers. The number of voltage droppers you need depends on the voltage of the AC source. If your power pack supplies 17 to 18 volts, use three. If it supplies 20 volts, use four. If you use a transformer that has a fixed or maximum output of 13 volts, such as Radio Shack's AC to AC adapter for answering machines (273-1610A), you can do without the voltage dropper bank entirely. If you are using the AC to AC adapter, skip down to "Prepare the AC to AC adapter," below.

Take a moment to examine a rectifier. Its layout is somewhat

PARTS, MATERIALS, AND TOOLS

Parts

Two 1-K, 1-watt resistors (271-153). These resistors are wired to operate like a single 500-ohm, 2-watt resistor. Although this assembly should not present any problems, a single 470-ohm, 5-watt resistor (Digi-Key 470W-5ND; Hosfelt 5W-470; Mouser 28PR004-470) will provide a greater margin of security.

TIP 3055 NPN power transistor (276-2020)

Zero to five 2- to 4-amp, 50-PIV bridge rectifiers (276-1146). Radio Shack sells 4-amp units; 2-amp units are available from Hosfelt (KPB-204) and Digi-Key (BR81D-ND). See text.

Zero to five IN4001 1-amp, 50-PIV diodes (276-1101). See text. Radio Shack also sells an assortment of 25 1-amp diodes with various PIVs from 50 upward (276-1653).

Two IN4003, 1-amp diodes with a PIV of 200 or more (276-1102 or 276-1653)

Two 1000-µF, 35-volt electrolytic capacitors with radial leads (272-1032)

One 4700-µF, 35- or 50-volt electrolytic capacitor with axial leads (272-1022)

0.1-µF, 200- or 250-volt capacitors (272-1053; Digi-Key EF2104-ND; Mouser 146-250V.1K). Two to four per switch. Optional, but desirable. Described in the text.

Two 2-position barrier strips (274-656)

HO or N gauge power pack. Make sure it has AC accessory terminals. You can also use an old Marx transformer with a maximum output of 13 volts or Radio Shack's AC to AC adapter for answering machines (273-1610), which has the same output. Devices with a DC output will not work. This circuit must have its own power source; it cannot be powered from the fixed-voltage terminal of the transformer that supplies the track.

6-amp momentary, center off, SPDT switch (Hosfelt 51-219; Mouser 10TC245; Jameco 75889). This switch is intended to replace the original switch controller and can be mounted in a ¼" hole. You can also use Radio Shack's 20-amp momentary center off, DPDT switch (275-709) or two 3-amp push buttons (275-1556).

Machine screws, nuts, and lock washers. These differ according to the type of switch. Radio Shack sells some of the specified screws and nuts, but not the lock washers, which you will have to get at a hardware store or hobby shop.

Materials

18 gauge solid wire (278-1217 or 278-1223)

22 gauge stranded wire (278-1218 or 278-1224)

22 gauge solid wire (278-1215 or 278-1221)

24 gauge solid wire (278-1509). This is two-conductor speaker wire. The conductors can be pulled apart. You can also use two-conductor intercom wire (278-857). Single-conductor wire is available from Digi-Key (C2003B-100-ND).

.032 rosin-core solder (64-005)

Damp sponge

Medium-grade sandpaper

Silicone sealant (64-2314)

Plastic tray from a microwave dinner. Get one that is not divided into separate compartments.

Videocassette labels (44-1103) or dry transfers

Regular (slow-setting) epoxy, for modifying later Marx switches (64-2313)

Electrical tape (64-2340, 64-2353, or 64-2348)

1⁄16" or 3⁄32" heat-shrink tubing (278-1627)

Tools

15- to 25-watt soldering pencil (64-2051 or 64-2070)

Heavy-duty (50- to 100-watt soldering gun) (64-2193)

Needle-nose pliers (64-1812 or 64-1844)

Wire stripper/cutter (64-1952 or 64-2129)

Helping Hands or similar project holder (64-2093)

Paper clips: one small 1¼" paper clip, and one large (2") vinyl-coated paper clip. Straighten both paper clips.

Hair dryer

Small slotted screwdriver

Medium-size slotted screwdriver

Soldering heatsink (276-1567)

The following tools are needed for modifying Lionel switches, as required by the circuit.

Hammer

Nail set

Hobby tool and aluminum oxide or silicon carbide grinding wheel. To modify later Marx switches, you will also need a cutting disk for the hobby tool.

Safety goggles for use with the hobby tool

Small file

Drill and bits up to about ¼"

different from the units used in earlier chapters. The end leads are the DC terminals, and the positive lead is usually longer than the others. Note that the positive lead of a bridge rectifier is identical to the cathode of a diode. Trim the leads of the rectifier to about ½", and clamp it in the Helping Hands, leads facing up.

Take a diode and make two or three closely spaced loops in the ends of the leads by winding them on the large paper clip. Bend the leads so that the loops will fit onto the end terminals of the rectifier, as shown in fig. 5-4. Push the lead onto the rectifier terminals, cathode (banded end) to the negative terminal of the rectifier, and squeeze them tight with the needle-nose pliers.

Now solder each diode lead to its rectifier lead. Because of the thickness of the rectifier leads, you will probably have to use a heavy-duty soldering gun, and you will need a large heatsink: for a heatsink, wrap a wide rubber band around the handles of a pair of needle-nose pliers to hold them closed. Clamp them onto the rectifier lead between the joint and the case. Attach a small soldering heatsink to the diode lead between the joint and the diode, and solder the joint.

For the first voltage dropper, cut a 3" piece of 24 gauge wire and strip ½" from the ends. For each additional unit, cut a 2" piece and strip its ends. Clamp the first voltage dropper in the Helping Hands, leads pointing up. With the large paper clip, coil one end of the 3" wire. Push the coiled end onto an AC (middle) terminal of the rectifier and squeeze it tight. Attach the needle-nose pliers and solder the joint. Following this procedure, attach a 2" piece of wire to each additional voltage dropper.

Now solder the rectifiers together. Each 2" wire goes to the remaining AC terminal on the

Fig. 5-6. The Resistor Assembly

neighboring rectifier, as shown in fig. 5-5. When you have finished, there should be one free 3" wire attached to one rectifier and one unused AC terminal on another. Solder a second 3" wire to the unused terminal. Check to make sure that the diode and DC (end) leads do not touch any AC (center) leads. When you have soldered all the joints and checked everything, stack the rectifiers so that the front of one faces the rear of another (see fig. 5-5).

Prepare the AC to AC adapter, if you are using one. Cut the plug off the low-voltage output cord, and separate the two conductors for about 2". Then strip ½" from the ends and tin them.

Prepare the resistor assembly. Coil the ends of the leads of one resistor, and slip each coiled end onto a lead of the other resistor, as shown in fig. 5-6. Squeeze the coils tight and solder them.

Prepare the transistor. Bend the leads up at right angles, about ⅛" from the case.

Prepare the barrier strips. Loosen all the screws. It is easier to do this now than later.

Mount the parts. With silicone sealant, mount the parts, except for the resistor assembly and the remaining diodes, on the microwave dinner tray. For suggested layout, see figs. 5-1 and 5-2. Pay special attention to the locations of the positive and negative capac-

itor leads. Add the videotape labels as indicated.

WIRE THE CIRCUIT

When you wire the circuit, refer to figs. 5-1 and 5-2. Use 24 gauge solid wire.

❑ Attach one 3" wire from the voltage dropper bank to the upper terminal of the AC barrier strip. Wrap the wire around the screw and lower the screw into its hole before you tighten it.

If you do not require a voltage dropper bank, strip ½" from each end of a 3" length of wire. Then coil one end with the small paper clip and screw the other end into the upper terminal of the AC barrier strip.

❑ Join the middle leads of capacitors C1 and C2 together. Twist one lead around the other, leaving ¼" of one lead sticking up. Note that the upper lead must be negative and the lower lead, positive. Solder the connection.

❑ Strip ½" from the end of the other 3" wire from the voltage dropper bank, and coil the end with the small paper clip. Push the coiled end onto the lead at the junction of capacitors C1 and C2. Squeeze the connection with needle-nose pliers to make sure it is firm. Then solder it. Whenever you solder a connection, squeeze it tight first, if possible. If you do not require a voltage dropper bank, solder the wire from the upper AC terminal directly to the junction of capacitors C1 and

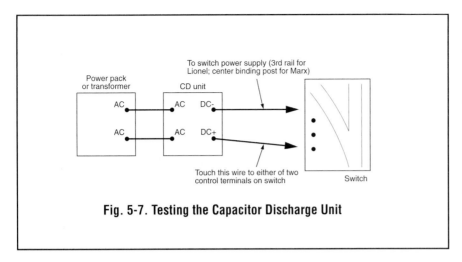

Fig. 5-7. Testing the Capacitor Discharge Unit

C2. This wire is shown by a dotted line in fig. 5-2. Push the coiled end of the wire onto the capacitor lead, and solder it.

❏ Join diode D2 to the positive lead of capacitor C1. With the small paper clip, make two or three loops in the cathode lead (to the banded end) of diode D2. Push it onto the positive (upper) lead of capacitor C1, and solder it about ¼" from the capacitor case. Don't forget the soldering heatsink on the lead, between the joint and the diode. Don't trim the capacitor lead down to the joint yet.

❏ Join diode D2 to diode D1. Coil the end of the cathode lead (to the banded end) of diode D1. Push it onto the anode lead of diode D2 and solder it ¼" from the case. Leave a ¼" piece of lead sticking out from the joint.

❏ Coil the end of the anode lead of diode D1. Push it onto the negative (lower) lead of capacitor C2, and solder it about ¼" from the case. Again, don't trim the capacitor lead down to the joint.

❏ Run a wire from the junction of diodes D1 and D2 to the lower terminal of the AC barrier strip, and strip ½" from both ends. Coil one end. Push it onto the ¼" lead at the junction of the diodes, and solder it. Screw the other end into the lower barrier strip terminal.

❏ Install the resistor assembly. Coil both ends of the resistor assembly. Push one end onto the positive (upper) lead of capacitor C1 and solder the joint. Leave a ¼" piece of lead from the capacitor or resistor assembly. Push the other end of the resistor assembly onto the base (left-hand terminal) of transistor and solder it. The transistor, like the diodes, requires using the soldering heatsink. Leave enough of the base terminal to make room for another connection.

❏ Add the collector connection. Run a wire to the collector (center terminal) of the transistor from the junction of the resistor assembly and the positive lead of capacitor C1. Coil each end of the wire. Solder one end to the ¼" piece of capacitor or resistor lead, and the other to the collector (center terminal) of the transistor. If necessary, bend the end transistor leads apart.

❏ Add the emitter connection. Run a wire from the emitter (right-hand terminal) of the transistor to the positive terminal of capacitor C3. Coil the ends of the wire, push each end onto its terminal, and solder it. Don't trim the capacitor lead yet.

❏ Prepare the protection diodes D7 and D8. Coil the end of the cathode lead (to the banded end) of diode D8. Clamp diode D7 in the

Helping Hands. Push the coiled end of the cathode lead of diode D8 onto the anode lead of diode D7 and solder it about ¼" from the case of diode D7.

❏ Attach the protection diodes to capacitor C3. Coil the end of the anode lead of diode D7, and solder it to the positive lead of capacitor C3.

❏ Connect the base (of the transistor) to the cathode lead (to the banded end) of diode D7. Run a wire from the base (left-hand terminal) of the transistor to the cathode lead (to the banded end) of diode D7. Coil the ends of the wire, push them on to the leads, and solder them. The diode connection should be ¼" from the case.

❏ Connect capacitors C2 and C3 to protection diode D8. Run a wire from negative lead of capacitor C2 to the negative lead of capacitor C3 and from there to the anode lead of diode D8. When you strip and coil the ends of the wire, also strip and coil a ½" section in the middle, where the negative lead of capacitor C3 will be attached. Push the coiled sections onto the leads and solder them. The connection to diode D8 should be ¼" from the case.

❏ Attach the cathode lead of diode D7 to the upper terminal of the DC barrier strip (BS-2). Wrap the lead around the screw and lower it into the hole. If the leads in this and the following step are too short to attach to the barrier strip, splice pieces of wire to them.

❏ Attach the anode lead of diode D8 to the lower terminal of the DC barrier strip (BS-2). Follow the same procedure as in the preceding step.

❏ Trim any excess leads or wires from the solder joints.

TEST AND INSTALL THE CIRCUIT

Test the circuit. First check to see that all the connections and polarities are correct. Most of the components in this circuit are polarized and must be connected properly. Make sure that neighboring points do not touch each other. If the joints or leads are too close together, use a small screwdriver to push them apart.

You will now need a remote-control switch. Unscrew the switch motor cover, and remove the bulb to prevent it from burning out. Following fig. 5-7, connect the two terminals of the AC barrier strip to the AC terminals of a power pack or suitable transformer. Next run a wire from one DC output terminal to the common connection of the switch. On unmodified Lionel switches, this will be the third rail. On Marx switches, it will be the center binding post. Finally connect a wire to the other DC output terminal, but leave it unattached.

Plug the power pack in and touch the unattached wire to one of two control terminals on the switch. On Marx switches, Lionel prewar switches, and 1121 units, these are the end binding posts. On Lionel 1122 switches, they are the two binding posts farthest from the switch machine. Each binding post feeds current to a solenoid and throws the switch. The switch should operate smartly with a snap. If one terminal doesn't work, wait five seconds or so and try the other. If, after touching both terminals, you see only some weak sparks and no motion, the capacitor is not charging. Look for an open connection or short circuit somewhere and correct it.

The capacitor requires about two seconds to recharge. If you move the unattached wire from one binding post to the other too quickly, the capacitor will not charge, and the switch will not work.

Prepare the switches. The amount and kind of preparation your switches require vary according to their type.

Lionel O27 switches. Lionel's 1121 and 1122 models (along with their MPC and LTI remakes) must be converted to fixed-voltage operation. Ray Plummer has presented a brief, illustrated account of how to do this, and I have incorporated some of his suggestions here.

The procedure for modifying 1122 switches is as follows (see fig. 5-8).
❑ Remove the detachable hardware. Remove the switch lantern and unscrew the switch motor housing. Remove the bulb.
❑ Remove the bottom cover plate. Turn the switch upside down and support it firmly on one or more pieces of wood. With a small screwdriver, carefully straighten out the tabs holding the rails on. If some of the tabs are also soldered on, use the desoldering braid and soldering gun to free them. Be careful not to damage the plastic base. Early 1122s have small pieces of rail that will probably fall down when you straighten out the tabs. Put them aside in a margarine tub or similar container.

On early 1122s, the frog point (the triangle at the junction of the straight and curved rails) is secured to the bottom cover plate by a drive screw. Remove the drive screw, which looks like a screw without a slot or threads, by driving it out from the top with a hammer and a nail set. Put aside the drive screw and the frog point.

Instead of a separate drive screw, later 1122s have a stud molded into the frog point. Turn the switch upside down and use a hobby tool with a silicon carbide or aluminum oxide grinding wheel to grind this stud down to the bottom cover plate. Use a hammer and a nail set to drive the frog point out. Then put the frog point aside.

Turn the switch right side up. You will see two rivets at one end of the switch machine on a metal plate. The rivet at the center of this plate goes all the way through the bottom cover plate. Grind the end of this rivet down to the switch machine plate.

Make sure the switch is firmly supported, so that nothing will bend or break. Support the area directly under the rivet with a small piece of wood in which you have drilled a ¼" hole. Center the rivet directly over the hole, so that the rivet will fall into the hole when you drive it out.

Now with a hammer and nail set, drive the rivet out. If it won't come right out, grind it down some more.

At this point, up to three rivets remain, holding the bottom cover plate on. Early switches have two rivets at either end and one that forms the base of the ground binding post stud. Later switches lack the end rivets but still have the holes originally intended for them. Turn the switch upside down and remove the two end rivets the same way you removed the first rivet. Then grind down the bottom of the binding post stud. If possible, grind it to the point where you can lift the cover plate off without disturbing the stud. If you can't lift off the cover plate, just grind the stud down and drive it out. Save the binding post nut.

Now the cover plate should come off, together with a special sheet of insulating paper. On the switch base, mark exactly where this sheet fits. Save the sheet, and be careful not to damage it. Put the sheet and the bottom cover plate aside.
❑ Disconnect the solenoids from the third rail. First, examine the bottom of the switch, and note where the solenoid leads go. One lead from each solenoid is soldered to a sheet-steel strip that is connected to a binding post and an insulated running rail. The remaining two leads are twisted together and soldered to a copper strip that is connected to the third rail. The copper strip also powers the switch lamp. All four leads are simply pieces of thin magnet wire unwound from the solenoids. Be

very careful when you work with them. Although they may be protected by cloth sleeves, these wires break easily and are difficult to repair.

Now unsolder the leads from the copper strip. To protect the switch base from heat damage, slide a piece of cardboard under the strip at the solder joint.

❏ Attach the new wire or wires. Carefully splice the unsoldered leads to a foot of 22 gauge stranded wire as follows. Strip ½" from the end of the 22 gauge wire and coil it with the small paper clip. Then slide it onto the solenoid leads, squeeze the joint with needle-nose pliers, and solder it. To minimize the chances of damage to the solenoid leads, immediately attach the soldered joint and leads to the plastic switch base with electrical tape.

Cover the joint completely with electrical tape, and make sure that no bare wire or solder joint touches any other metal in the switch. Once immobilized and protected with tape, the leads should be safe.

While the bottom cover plate is off, you might consider using the opportunity to rewire the switch lamp so that it can be powered from a separate transformer. Normally,

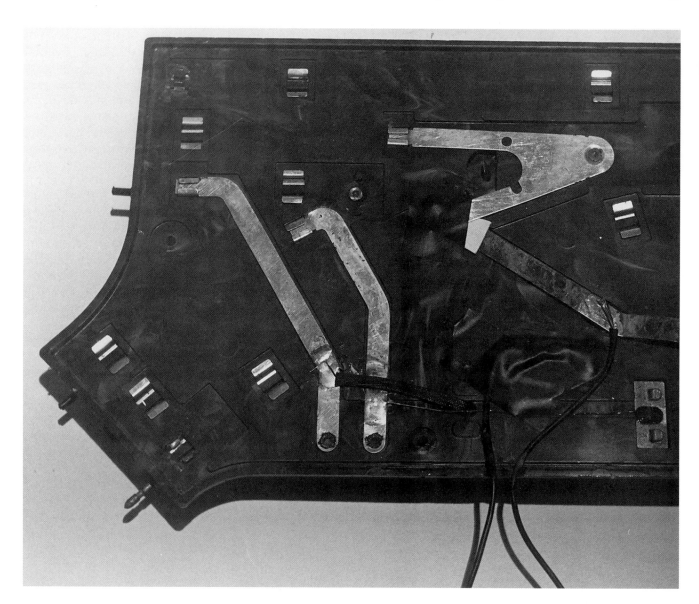

Fig. 5-8. A Modified 1122 Switch with the Bottom Cover Plate Removed. The right-hand wire is attached to the copper strip that powers the lamp. The copper strip is insulated from track voltage by a piece of cardboard at the center. The left-hand wire is soldered to solenoid leads under the electrical tape. Note the remaining solenoid leads, which are soldered to strips attached to the binding posts and the insulated running rails.

one end of the copper strip forms a terminal contact for the lightbulb, while the other end fits under a sheet-steel strip held in place by tabs from the third rail. In this arrangement, track voltage powers the lightbulb. If you have several switches whose indicator lamps are powered by track voltage, the extra current demand can slow the train and overload the transformer. Powering the switch lamps from a separate transformer reduces the load on the main transformer, makes troubleshooting easier, and facilitates the installation of future electronic circuitry. If you wish to continue powering the indicator lamp from track voltage, skip down to "Prepare the switch for reassembly," below.

In order to power the switch lamp with a separate transformer, you must disconnect the lamp circuit from the third rail and install a separate feeder wire. With a pencil, trace a line on the copper strip where the copper strip passes under the sheet-steel strip. Then gradually work the copper strip out. Use a hobby tool and cutting disk to cut out most of the section that had been under the sheet-steel strip. But leave a small tab that will still fit under it. At the spot on the copper strip where the solenoid leads had been attached, solder a foot of 22 gauge stranded wire. Label this wire and the wire to the switch machines.

Reinstall the copper strip, sliding the tab under the sheet-steel strip. Slide a piece of thin cardboard between the tab and the sheet-steel strip so that the cardboard completely separates the two. Test the circuit as follows: Connect a transformer to the third rail and to a running rail. The lightbulb should not go on. If the bulb goes on, move the cardboard strip until it goes out. Now connect the transformer to the wire

attached to the copper strip and to a running rail. This time the lightbulb should go on. Tape the cardboard in place.

If you also need to disconnect the nonderailing feature, now is the time to do it.

The nonderailing feature consists of two sheet-steel strips. One end of each strip is connected to a solenoid via a binding post, while the other end is connected to an insulated running rail. When a train passes over, it grounds the running rail, throwing the switch in the proper direction.

To disconnect this feature, carefully straighten out the tabs securing each strip to its insulated rail. Then wrap the end of the strip with electrical tape so that there is no longer an electrical connection between the strip and the rail. Replace the strip and bend the tabs back into place.

Now connect two wires to a transformer and turn it on. Touch one wire to a strip and one to the tab securing its insulated rail. There should not be a spark. If there is, you will have to retape the end of the strip. Repeat this procedure with the other strip.

❏ Prepare the switch for reassembly. For each wire, file or grind a notch in the edge of the plastic switch base in front of the solenoids. Fit the switch onto its bottom cover plate, and at the notch make a mark on the edge of the cover plate. Remove the cover plate. At the mark make a notch in the cover plate. Fit the switch onto the cover plate again to make sure the notches meet and form a hole through which the wire can pass without being squeezed.

❏ Reassemble the switch. Feed each wire through its notch in the switch base. Carefully reinstall the insulating paper and the cover plate. For reattaching the cover plate, replace the three rivets with 2-56 x ¼" (64-3010) roundhead

machine screws with locknuts (64-3017) and lock washers. Push the screws in from underneath, and then attach the washers and nuts. If you had to drill out the ground binding post stud, replace it with a 4-40 x ½" flathead machine screw, locknut, and washer. A roundhead screw (64-3011) will work, but it will protrude slightly from the bottom. Reinstall the binding post nut.

If you can't screw the binding post nut onto your 4-40 machine screw, don't fret. The threads vary, and sometimes the nuts don't fit. Get a 4-40 tap from the hardware store. Hold the tap, which looks like a threaded drill bit, with a pair of pliers. Oil the threads and insert the tap into the top of the binding post nut. Carefully screw it into the nut, until the nut turns freely. The tap will cut some metal from the threads, and afterwards the nut should fit the binding post without any trouble.

❏ Reinstall the frog point. If your switch has a separate drive screw, use a nail set and hammer to reinstall the drive stud and the frog point in the switch. If your switch has a frog point with a built-in stud, snap it back into place. If the frog point is loose, you can secure it to the switch base (not the bottom cover plate) with epoxy. Use a regular (slow-setting) epoxy. Reinstall any pieces of rail that came out, and carefully bend the tabs back in place.

❏ Reinstall the remaining hardware. Reinstall the lightbulb, the switch machine cover, and the indicator lantern.

The procedure for modifying Lionel's older 1121 switches is similar, but somewhat simpler. Refer to figs. 5-9 and 5-10.

❏ Remove the detachable hardware. Unscrew the switch machine cover, and remove the bulb.

❏ Remove the bottom cover plate. Instead of rivets, four eyelets hold

Fig. 5-9. A Modified 1121 Switch, with Switch Machine Cover Removed. The upper wire powers the lamp, while the lower wire powers the solenoids.

the cover plate on. These can be removed in much the same way as the rivets in the 1122 switch. Turn the switch upside down and support it. With a hobby tool, grind the edges of the eyelets down. Then drill the eyelets out with a 9/64" or 5/32" bit. When you remove the bottom cover plate, save the sheet of insulating paper.

❏ Disconnect the lamp. Examine the switch, and trace the power wire to its connection with the third rail. Although the circuitry of the 1121 switch is identical to that of the 1122, the actual wiring is a little different. The lamp wire and the power wire from the third rail are connected to the junction of the solenoid leads. In order to power the switch with a CD unit,

the lamp wire must be rerouted either to its own connection with the third rail, or (better) to its own power supply. Otherwise, the light-bulb will drain so much current from the CD unit that the capacitor will not charge.

Trace the lamp wire and clip it about 2" from the light socket. This wire is soldered to an eyelet in a fiber disk at the bottom of the socket. Push the wire and the disk out, and unsolder the wire from the eyelet; clamp the disk in the Helping Hands. Hold the soldering gun against the eyelet, and pull on the wire with pliers until it comes loose. Discard the wire, but hold onto the disk.

Tape the end of the lamp wire still attached to the solenoid leads,

since you will not be using it. Do not try to disconnect this wire from the solenoid leads, as they are delicate and break easily.

If you plan to power the lamp from the third rail, cut a piece of 22 gauge stranded wire long enough to reach the solder joint on the third rail. If you plan to power the lamp from a separate transformer, cut a piece a foot long. Now attach one end of the wire to the eyelet in the fiber disk as follows.

Clamp the disk in the Helping Hands, and tin the end of the wire. Tin the eyelet, filling it with solder. Trim the tinned end of the wire to about 1/16". With the soldering gun or pencil, heat the solder in the eyelet, and push the wire in from the other side. Hold the wire still

68

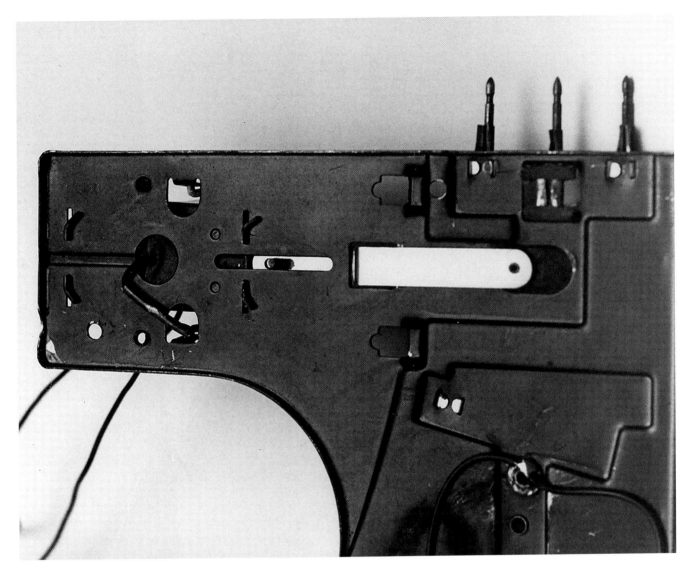

Fig. 5-10. A Modified 1121 Switch, with Bottom Cover Plate Removed. The power wire is connected to the solenoid leads at center left.

until the solder hardens. Trim any excess wire sticking out through the disk. Reinstall the disk and wire assembly in its socket. Make sure that the insulation goes all the way up to the eyelet, and that neither bare wire nor solder touches the metal socket. Leave the other end of the lamp wire unattached for the time being.

❑ Unsolder the power wire for the switch machines from the third rail and attach the new wire. If the power wire is in good shape, cut it down to about 2", and splice the end to a foot of 22 gauge stranded wire. Work carefully to avoid disturbing the delicate solenoid windings to which the power wire is attached. Strip about ¼" from the end of the power wire, and sand it until it is clean and bright. Then use the small paper clip to coil the end of the new piece of wire. Push the coiled end onto the end of the power wire, squeeze it tight with pliers, and solder it. Slide a piece of ¹⁄₁₆" or ³⁄₃₂" heat-shrink tubing over the splice, and shrink it in place with a hair dryer. Tape the splice in place, so that it won't move. Then feed the wire up through the switch base next to the solenoids.

If the insulation is brittle or cracked, follow the procedure indicated above. But use a piece of heat-shrink tubing long enough to cover both the splice and the bad insulation. After you solder the wires, carefully solder the heat-shrink tubing over the joint and the old wire, to the junction with the solenoid leads if possible. Then shrink the tubing, tape the splice

69

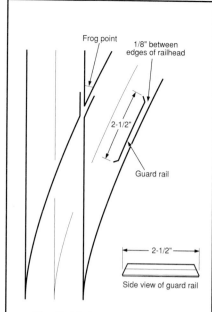

Fig. 5-11. Installation of Guard Rail on Later Marx Switches

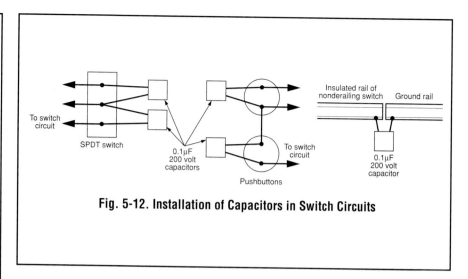

Fig. 5-12. Installation of Capacitors in Switch Circuits

in place, and feed the wire up through the switch base.

If you intend to power the switch lamp from track voltage, solder the lamp wire to the spot on the third rail to which the power wire for the switch machine had been attached.

If you intend to provide a separate power source for the switch lamp, label the free ends of the lamp wire and the switch machine power wire.

If you have an older 1121 switch, inspect the wires joining the three sections of third rail, and replace them if they are broken or if their insulation is cracked.

❏ Prepare the switch for reassembly. To provide an opening for the new wire or wires, file a notch in the bottom of the switch machine cover.

❏ Reassemble the switch. Dress the wires, making sure that they do not interfere with any moving parts. Replace the insulating paper, and fit the bottom cover plate onto the switch. To secure the

bottom cover plate to the switch, use ¼" 6-32 flat-head machine screws with locknuts (64-3018) and lock washers. Insert the screws in the holes from which you removed the eyelets, pushing them in from underneath. Finally, replace the bulb, and screw on the switch machine cover.

Marx O27 switches. Early Marx switches (all metal) require no modification.

Late Marx switches (with a plastic base) require no modification in wiring. However, for most modern engines, they must have a guard rail installed next to the curve rail, across from the frog (fig. 5-11). Otherwise, these engines will ride up the frog and derail. To determine whether you need a guard rail, first test the switch with an engine.

To install the guard rail, cut a 2½" piece from the outermost rail of a section of O27 curved track. Cut the ends at an angle, away from the top of the rail, as shown in fig. 5-11. Bend the cut ends of the section slightly, away from the curve, and sand the bottom bright. Mix a batch of slow-setting epoxy and attach the guard rail to the switch base next to the curved rail. Make sure that a ⅛" gap separates the inside edges of each

railhead (the round top of the rail).

O gauge switches. Tabs on the base of prewar Lionel 011 and 012 switches secure the bottom cover plate to the switch. These tabs break easily, and often the cover plate is missing, along with some or all of the wiring. If your switch still has its cover plate, carefully bend the tabs in order to remove it. If they break, you may be able to replace them with small sheet-metal screws installed in holes drilled in the edges of the cover plate and the base.

The wiring of 011 and 012 switches is virtually identical to that of the 1121s, and may be modified for CD units the same way.

Prewar American Flyer switches do not require modification.

Like 1121s, postwar Lionel 022 switches have a light whose power wire must be rerouted either to the third rail or to a separate power source. Unsolder the light wire from its connection with the constant-voltage plug. Then splice a length of 22 gauge stranded wire to it, and attach the lengthened wire to a connection with the third rail or a separate power supply. Insulate the splice with heat-shrink tubing. You will have to remove the indicator lightbulbs in the controller, since their current

70

drain will prevent the CD unit from charging.

Converting K-Line switches to CD power is not recommended because it requires doing without the indicator lights on both the controller and the switch machine. However, no modifications are necessary other than removal of the bulbs.

Install the circuit and the switches. Proper installation requires wire and switches of adequate capacity. For the power wire, use 18 gauge solid wire. For the control wires, use 22 gauge solid wire. If the switches are more than 35 feet from the CD unit, use 18 gauge wire for everything.

If you have them, you can reuse the original controllers that came with your switches. But you must first remove the indicator bulbs. These bulbs, like those in the switch itself, will drain too much current from the circuit and prevent the capacitor from charging.

A better strategy is to use one of the switches in the parts list. Radio Shack's 20-amp switch (275-709) provides the greatest margin of security. But any of the 6-amp switches should be adequate. You can also use two 3-amp push buttons. Avoid 0.5-amp push buttons and HO switch controllers. Although at first they appear to work properly, their contacts eventually heat up and burn out.

To extend the life of the switch contacts, install 0.1-microfarad, 200-volt capacitors between the center terminal and each of the end terminals of each SPDT switch. If you are using push buttons, install the capacitors between the terminals of each push button (fig. 5-12).

Besides extending the life of the switch contacts, the capacitors suppress unwanted radio emissions or "noise," which can disturb the operation of other electronic circuitry. Capacitors should also be installed between a ground rail

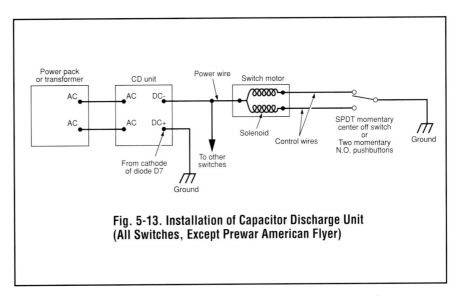

Fig. 5-13. Installation of Capacitor Discharge Unit (All Switches, Except Prewar American Flyer)

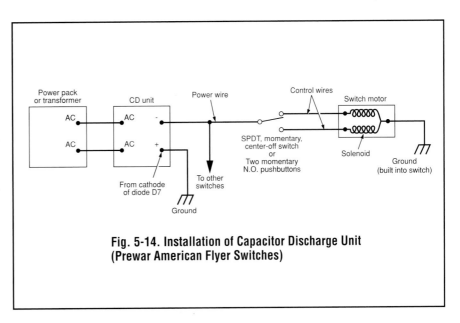

Fig. 5-14. Installation of Capacitor Discharge Unit (Prewar American Flyer Switches)

and the insulated running rails of nonderailing switches. When you install the capacitors, keep their leads as short as possible.

Wire all switches, except prewar American Flyer units, according to fig. 5-13. Note that grounding a control wire throws the switch by energizing the solenoid to which it is connected. Connect the power (hot) wire to the center binding post of Marx switches and to the constant voltage terminal of Lionel 022 and K-Line switches. In Lionel O27 switches, connect this wire to

the switch machine wire that you just installed. Be aware that early (all-metal) Marx switches consume considerably more current than other switches, and that the CD unit can power no more than one at a time.

To wire prewar American Flyer switches, which are thrown by connecting a solenoid to the power source, follow fig. 5-14. The ground connection is built into American Flyer switches, so that you need only connect the two control wires.

When you wire the switches, you can screw the lamp and switch machine wires into barrier strips. Or you can use wire nuts. Either method makes it much easier to attach other wires and to remove the accessory for repair than it would be if you soldered the connections. To use a wire nut, strip ½" from the ends of the wires, twist the ends together and screw on the wire nut.

If you power the switch lamps with a separate transformer (fig. 5-15), connect one of its terminals to the ground and the other to a power line of 18 gauge wire. Connect the feeder wires from the individual switch lamps to the power line. To reduce current consumption, use. no. 52 (screw-base) or no. 53 (bayonet) bulbs, at 10 to 12 volts. At that voltage, these bulbs consume about 0.1 amp each. A 35-watt O27 starter transformer can power about 20 bulbs.

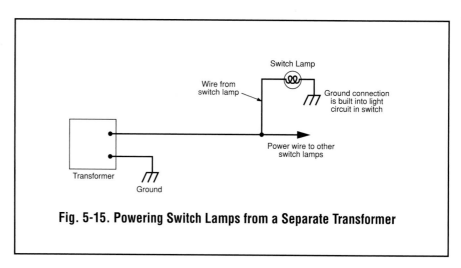

Fig. 5-15. Powering Switch Lamps from a Separate Transformer

6

Simple DC Directional Control

The next two chapters present two circuits: a simple DC directional control and a combination DC directional control and throttle. These devices will enable you to control the speed and direction of your engines more easily than existing tinplate circuitry. They are relatively uncomplicated and will make operation of your trains more reliable and trouble free.

HOW TOY TRAIN MOTORS WORK

Most Lionel locomotives have been powered by *universal motors*, i.e., motors that run on either AC or DC. A universal motor has a stationary coil, the *field coil*, and a rotating component, the *armature*, which consists of three or more coils on a laminated core. Centered on the armature is a segmented bronze disk, the *commutator*, on which two small cylinders, the *brushes*, ride. The brushes and commutator conduct electricity to the coils of the armature, as shown in fig. 6-1.

Electricity generates magnetic fields in the field coil and the coils of the armature. Together, the brushes and commutator act as a switch, alternating the connections to the coils of the armature

and thus changing its magnetic field. The changes in the magnetic field of the armature cause it to rotate as each pole is pulled, one after the other, through the magnetic field of the field coil.

The relationship of the armature and field coil determines the direction in which the armature rotates.

In a universal motor, it is necessary to switch the external connections to the armature or the field coil in order to change that relationship and reverse the motor. To switch these connections, Lionel first used a manual disk switch. Later, the company replaced the switch with its E-unit, a

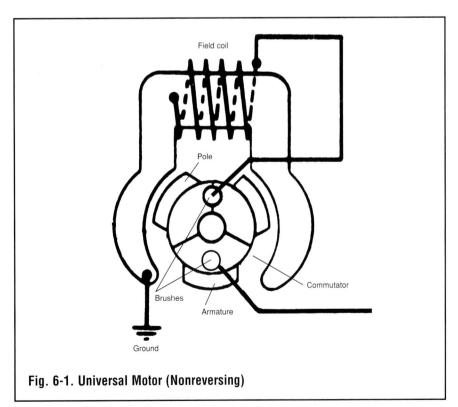

Field coil

Pole

Commutator

Brushes

Armature

Ground

Fig. 6-1. Universal Motor (Nonreversing)

Fig. 6-2. A Three-Position E-Unit

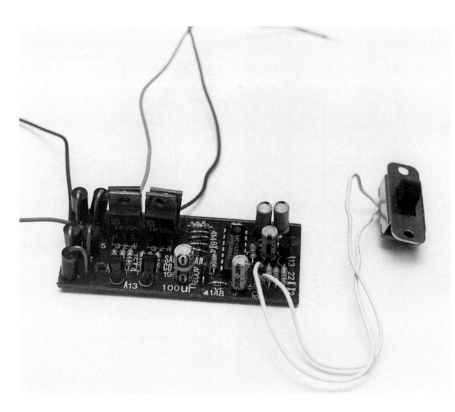

Fig. 6-3. An Electronic E-Unit from a K-Line Engine

relay triggered by interruptions in the track current (see fig. 6-2).

Originally developed by Ives, the E-unit has not been trouble free. In its long history, it has probably caused more frustration than any other single device. It tends to trip whenever dirt interrupts the track current. Its contacts and drum are vulnerable to wear and oxidation. And its open construction exposes it to dirt, oil, and grease, all of which interfere with its operation.

Instead of a field coil, a DC motor uses a powerful permanent magnet, whose magnetic field is unaffected by changes in current. As a result, reversing the current is sufficient to change the relationship between the magnet and the armature coils and thus reverse the rotor.

To reverse the current, only a simple DPDT switch is required. That is the great advantage of a DC permanent magnet motor: nothing else is needed to reverse it. It makes the E-unit, with all its problems, unnecessary.

WHY AC IS STILL WITH US

The benefits of DC polarity reverse have been known for some time. American Flyer, in fact, brought out a DC line in 1947. However, the critical components needed for successful DC operation—small powerful magnets and inexpensive, compact rectifiers—did not exist then, and in 1950 American Flyer abandoned its DC line.

Much later, in the 1970s and 1980s, when the necessary parts were available, Lionel made several DC starter sets. But by that time, the toy train market had changed. A growing segment consisted of older collectors and operators who wanted new equipment to be compatible with what they already had. And Lionel continued to design its more expensive equipment for AC. So AC survived, along with the universal motor and the temperamental E-unit.

However, the efficiency and low cost of DC can motors were too great for manufacturers to ignore, and eventually a compromise emerged: new equipment that was powered by DC can motors, but equipped with electronic E-units (fig. 6-3), which allowed the motors to run on AC.

The new E-units, with their solid-state circuitry, are considerably more reliable than the old. But they remain awkward to use. Even E-units programmed to ignore momentary interruptions in the track current still do not permit easy, reliable, directional control. For, like their predecessors, they are triggered by current interruptions. For the most part, it is still impossible simply to stop the train and restart it in the same direction without first disconnecting the E-unit. It is impossible, that is, without installing resistors or other devices that leak just enough current to keep the E-unit engaged, but not enough to drive the motor. Trainmaster, Lionel's radio-control system, remedies this problem without requiring any modification of the engine. But while some operators may find radio control a satisfactory solution, it is expensive, and it still does not eliminate the operational problems of existing E-units.

The alternative is to get rid of the E-unit entirely, and that is what this chapter is about. The circuitry is simple, requiring only a few inexpensive components. But it makes a big difference.

RETROFITTING UNIVERSAL MOTORS

One problem remains: what to do with all the universal motors that still power tinplate locomotives. Changing the polarity of the current will not, by itself, change the direction of the motor, because

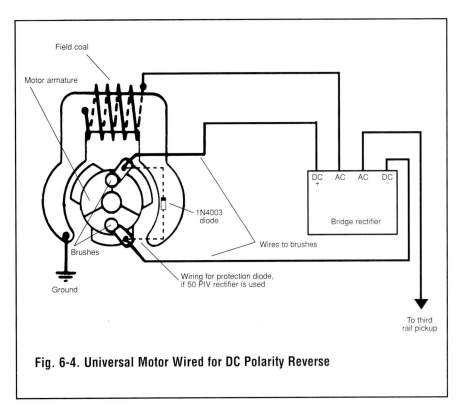

Fig. 6-4. Universal Motor Wired for DC Polarity Reverse

the relationship between the field coil and the armature remains unchanged. The problem is to find some way to convert a universal motor into a DC motor.

The solution is a bridge rectifier with its DC leads connected either to the brush terminals or, when one brush is the ground connection (as in the 1656 switcher), to the field coil terminals (fig. 6-4). No matter how current flows into the AC leads of the rectifier, it can only flow out of the DC leads one way. The rectifier keeps constant the direction of current flow and the resulting magnetic field. The end product is a reversible DC motor without a permanent magnet, a motor that makes directional control simple and trouble free.

The only disadvantage of DC operation is that it requires disconnecting onboard horns, whistles, and features such as Rail Sounds, which are triggered by a DC pulse. Otherwise, these devices will sound continuously. A simple, though per-

haps not ideal, solution is to mount these devices trackside, with their own circuits. It is also possible to purchase a commercial circuit that gives DC operators the same ability as AC operators to operate onboard horns and whistles.

PREPARE AND MOUNT THE PARTS

Mount the large bridge rectifier on its heatsink. Smear a thin coating of silicone heatsink grease (not sealant) on the back of the rectifier, and mount it on the heatsink with the 6-32 machine screw, lock washer, and locknut. Tighten the screw with a screwdriver and a wrench or a pair of pliers. If there is no hole in the center of the heatsink, you will have to drill one. The heatsink and rectifier should be mounted vertically to save space and dissipate heat into the air most efficiently.

Mount the parts of the main circuit board on the back of the microwave dinner tray. Before

PARTS, MATERIALS, AND TOOLS

Electronic parts

25-amp, 50-PIV bridge rectifier (276-1185). A rectifier with a PIV of 200 or higher is preferable and can be ordered from Digi-Key (MB252-ND) or Hosfelt (MB254). If you use a rectifier with the higher PIV, you will not need the next item.

IN4003 diode (276-1102) This protects the 50-PIV Radio Shack bridge rectifier from back emf originating in the motor.

One bridge rectifier for each motor unit. Use a 4-amp rectifier with a PIV of 200 or more (276-1173) for single-motor engines, and a 6- or 8-amp, 250-PIV rectifier for double-motor engines (276-1181). You can use rectifiers with a PIV of 50, but you will have to install a protection diode across their DC terminals or at the brush terminals.

4700-µF, 35-volt DC electrolytic capacitor (272-1022). This filters the rectified DC, improving motor performance. If you plan to operate only single motor engines, a 2200-µF capacitor (272-1020) should suffice. While this capacitor is not absolutely necessary for the simple directional circuit, you must install it if you plan to build the throttle described in the next chapter. Omitting the capacitor will make the motor run more slowly and less smoothly.

Other parts

Two 2-position barrier strips (274-656)

DPDT (double pole, double throw) switch with center off position and at least 10-amp contacts (275-1545 or 275-710). The 10-amp unit, which needs only a ¼" hole, is easier to install. The larger 20-amp unit, an automotive switch, is a bit easier to use but requires a larger hole to mount.

Heatsink for the bridge rectifier. I used a 16 gauge galvanized corner angle, measuring 3" x 2½" x 1¼", from the hardware store. Any similar sheet of steel or aluminum about this size will do. Look for a piece with a ⅛" hole in the middle for screwing in the rectifier, and a lip or flange that will permit it to be mounted vertically.

¾" 6-32 roundhead machine screw, with nut and lock washer for mounting the rectifier on the heatsink.

Female quick disconnects (64-3039). Optional. For attaching wires to the rectifier if you decide not to solder them. These are also called "push ons."

Terminal lugs. You can use Radio Shack's solderless ring tongues (64-3030). In spite of their name, they can be soldered.

Wire nuts (64-3057). The small and medium sizes seem to work best.

Materials

Silicone heatsink grease (276-1372)

Silicone rubber sealant (64-2314)

Electrical tape (64-2349)

.032 rosin-core solder (64-005)

Plastic tray from a microwave dinner, approximately 5" x 6". You can use another type of plastic, hardboard, or wood, as long as silicone sealant adheres to it.

Medium-grade sandpaper

Letters and numbers from a videotape label

Damp sponge

18 gauge solid wire (also called "bell wire") (278-1217 or 278-1223)

22 gauge stranded wire (278-1218 or 278-1224)

Tools

15- to 30-watt soldering pencil/gun (64-2802, 64-2066, or 64-2067)

50- to 100-watt soldering gun (64-2193)

Soldering heatsink (276-1567). Not to be confused with the heatsink on which the bridge rectifier will be mounted.

Medium-size screwdriver

Small (⅛") slotted screwdriver

Needle-nose pliers (64-1812 or 64-1844)

Flat-nose or electrician's pliers (64-1871)

Wire stripper/cutter (64-1952 or 64-2129)

Crimping tool 64-409 (optional). For joining wires to quick-disconnects instead of soldering them. This specialized tool works better than a combination wire stripper and crimper.

Small (1¼") paper clip. This and the following item are used for making loops in wire. Straighten both paper clips before using them.

Large (2") paper clip with plastic coating

Helping Hands (64-2093) or similar project holder

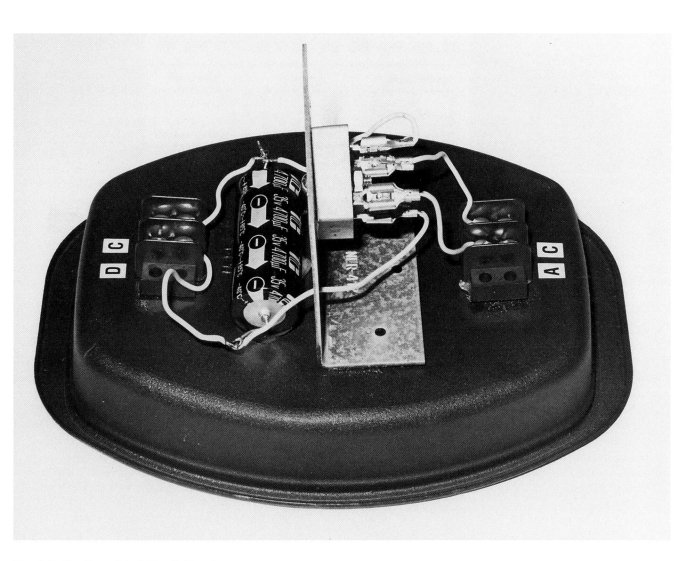

Fig. 6-5. The Completed Circuit Board

you mount the two barrier strips, loosen all the screws. Follow the layout in fig. 6-5, and mount the parts with silicone sealant. Do not mount the diode (if needed). Let the sealant cure overnight. Meanwhile, you can work on the DPDT switch and the engine rectifier.

Wire the DPDT switch. Take a moment to examine the switch and compare it with fig. 6-6. There are six terminals on the bottom. The two output leads from the circuit board are connected to the two center terminals, and the two leads to the track are connected to one pair of end terminals. Each end terminal is connected to the

end terminal diagonally opposite. If you trace the wires, you can see how throwing the switch reverses the connection, and thus the flow of current to the track. Note that in most of these switches, the circuit is closed between the center terminals and the terminals at the end opposite the direction in which the switch handle points.

Clamp the switch upside down in the Helping Hands. You will need four long pieces of 18 gauge solid wire. Two pieces must be long enough to go from the main circuit to the location of the switch (e.g., on a panel or box). The remaining two pieces must be long enough to

go from the location of the DPDT switch to the track or to a barrier strip connected to the track. In addition, you will need two short pieces of 18 gauge wire, long enough to connect the diagonal end terminals to each other. The 10-amp switch needs at least two inches, while the 20-amp switch needs at least three. Strip about ⅜" from the ends of all the long pieces of solid gauge wire.

Attach two of the long wires to the two middle terminals of the switch as follows: With the needle-nose pliers, bend one end of each wire into the shape of a V. Push it partway through the hole in the

77

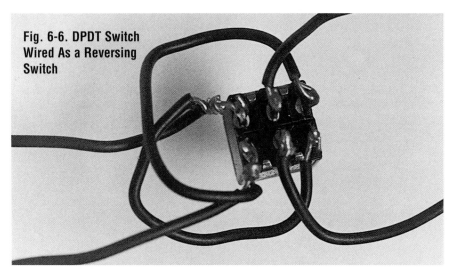

Fig. 6-6. DPDT Switch Wired As a Reversing Switch

the needle-nose pliers to tighten the loops and push them together. Push the coiled end of each wire onto one end of each of the remaining two unattached long wires, up to the insulation. Squeeze the joint tight with the needle-nose pliers.

Next, clamp the wires in the Helping Hands and solder them.

Attach each combination of wires to the switch: The end of the long wire to which the short wire is soldered goes to one corner terminal, while the other end of the short wire itself goes to the corner terminal diagonally opposite. Solder this wire to the switch the same way you soldered the first pair of wires to the middle terminals. Repeat the procedure with the other long wire and its attached short wire. Make sure that the long wires are soldered to terminals directly opposite each other.

Remove the cab or boiler from each engine. Before you can remove the E-unit, the cab or boiler must come off. With diesels

terminal, and then squeeze it with the pliers so that it is firmly in place. If the wire won't go through the hole, sand it a little. When you are satisfied that the connection is tight, solder it. You can use the soldering pencil with the small 10-amp switch, but you will need a soldering gun for the 20-amp unit. You can also attach the wires to

the 20-amp switch with quick-disconnects. Use a crimping tool to crimp the wires onto the disconnects. Then push the disconnects onto the switch terminals.

Strip about ¾" from the ends of the two short wires. Straighten the small paper clip, and wind one end of each wire around it, forming two or three tightly spaced loops. Use

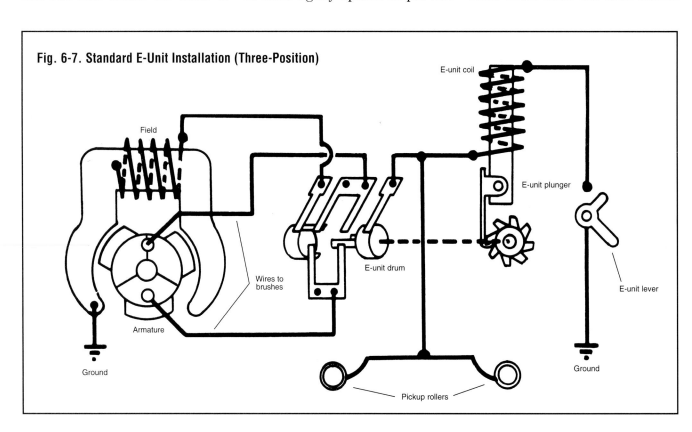

Fig. 6-7. Standard E-Unit Installation (Three-Position)

Field

E-unit coil

E-unit plunger

Wires to brushes

E-unit drum

E-unit lever

Armature

Ground

Ground

Pickup rollers

and electrics, you need only remove one or two screws to lift the cab off. On some units, you must also release the cab from a clip or tab. A few MPC engines whose railings fit into holes in the cab require an additional step: you must insert a 3 x 5 card between the cab and each railing. Otherwise the railings will scratch the cab.

Steam engines require a bit more work. To remove the boiler, you must take off the front and rear trucks, followed by the side rods, drive rods, and similar hardware. Next, you must take out the machine screws that secure the motor assembly to the boiler. At this point, you can usually lift the boiler off. (To keep track and to make reassembly easier, you may wish to consult the diagrams in Susan Pauker's *Greenberg's Repair & Operating Manual for Lionel Trains.* Jim Weatherford's videotapes are also helpful.)

Remove the E-unit from each engine. There are two kinds of E-units: the three-position E-unit and the two-position E-unit.

The three-position E-unit is the most common variety. It consists of a vertically mounted solenoid with a plastic drum and finger contacts at the bottom. (See fig. 6-2.) In a few rare instances, it is mounted horizontally. The three-position E-unit has a neutral setting as well as a forward and a reverse. Figure 6-7 shows wiring for engines with the three-position E-unit.

The two-position E-unit (fig. 6-8) is smaller than the three-position device and lacks a drum and finger contacts. It has only a forward and a reverse setting and is connected to a motor with two field coil windings, wound in opposite directions. By grounding one or the other winding the E-unit determines the direction in which the motor turns.

Lionel also used double-wound

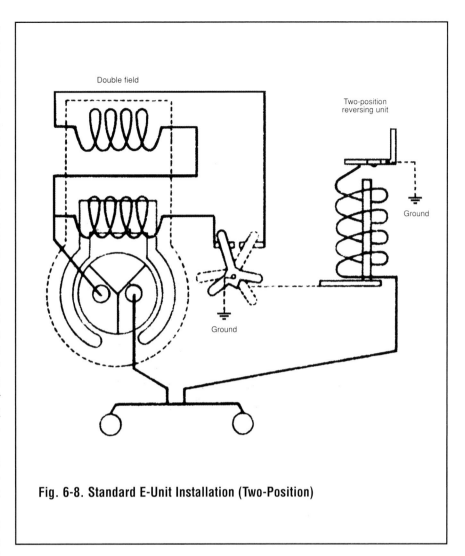

Fig. 6-8. Standard E-Unit Installation (Two-Position)

field coils with a manual SPDT switch that functioned in much the same way as the two-position E-unit, grounding either of the two field windings. Examine your motor's field coil. If it has more than two fine wires coming from it or if its wires are of two colors, it is a double-wound unit.

The first step is to unsolder the E-unit connections.

Three-position E-unit. The three-position E-unit has four wires, generally color coded. Two wires, most often yellow and blue, go from the E-unit to the brushes. A green wire goes from the E-unit to the field coil. (The solder lug to the field coil is usually between the

solder lugs to the brushes.) Some older engines have screw terminals on the brushplate, and instead of a separate field coil lug, a wire splice, covered with cloth insulation. A few engines (e.g., 1656) that are grounded through one brush connection have a single wire to the brushplate and two wires to the field coil. The fourth wire, usually black, is the hot wire to the third-rail pickup; it is attached to a solder lug on the E-unit itself. The headlight wire and the wire to the smoke generator, if any, are also attached to this lug.

Hold the hot soldering pencil or gun against each solder lug, so that the solder melts, and you can

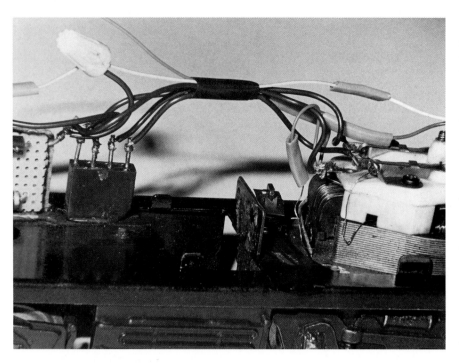

Fig. 6-9. Directional Rectifier Installed in an Engine. This motor has a double-wound field coil.

that were joined together. You will now see four fine wires, the two that had been twisted together and the two that had been separately connected to the E-unit terminals. Now connect two 22 gauge wires to the terminals of a transformer, and simultaneously touch each wire to the ends of two wires on either side of the field coil. If you get a spark, those two wires are from the same winding. If not, try again with another combination.

If you get no sparks, no matter what you do, the wires are broken somewhere, and you will have to locate the break and try to fix it. If, as is often the case, the break is on the top layer of the field coil, you might be able to unwind a length of wire beyond the break and connect it instead.

At this point, if there is no problem, one end of the remaining winding, which you will use in the circuit, should be still be connected to its solder lug, and the other end should be free.

Postwar engines with manual reverse. These engines have double-wound field coils and can be treated just like engines with two-position E-units. The only difference

pull the wire loose. Use the desoldering braid if necessary. The wires to the brushplate and the field coil lug will usually come off without too much trouble. The black hot wire, however, is often wrapped tightly around its lug on the E-unit along with the headlight and smoke generator wires, and sometimes these wires won't come loose without a struggle. If a 15- or 30-watt soldering pencil doesn't provide enough heat, you can use a 100-watt soldering gun. But you will have to work fast and be careful not to damage the area near the solder lug.

Two-position E-unit. Three wires are connected to solder lugs on the two-position E-unit. Two go to the field coil windings, and one goes to the third-rail pickup. Unsolder them, using the procedure outlined above for the three-position unit. Then unsolder and remove the wire connecting the field coil (center) lug to one brush terminal. Next seal off the ends of

one field coil winding with electrical tape, disconnecting it from the circuit.

If both windings use the same color wire, use the following procedure to tell them apart. Carefully unsolder and untwist the wires

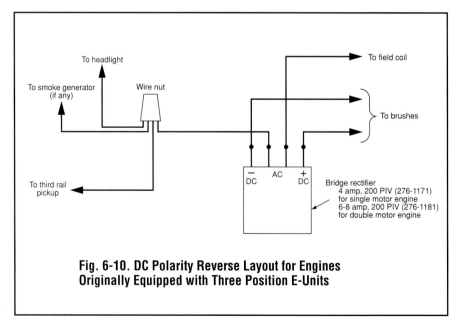

Fig. 6-10. DC Polarity Reverse Layout for Engines Originally Equipped with Three Position E-Units

80

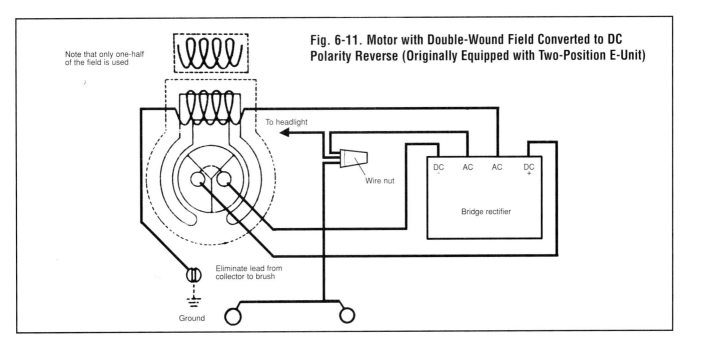

Fig. 6-11. Motor with Double-Wound Field Converted to DC Polarity Reverse (Originally Equipped with Two-Position E-Unit)

Note that only one-half of the field is used

To headlight

Wire nut

DC − AC AC DC +

Bridge rectifier

Eliminate lead from collector to brush

Ground

is that you must disconnect the reversing switch.

All that holds the E-unit on now is a screw on the side of the engine. Remove the screw, and you can take the E-unit out.

Prepare the engine rectifier for mounting. First consider where you want to mount the rectifier, bearing in mind that later on you may want to install other circuitry in the engine. I find it easiest to mount the rectifier and other circuitry vertically in a row, just inside the engine shell, as shown in fig. 6-9. Make sure that the rectifier has enough clearance so that its leads won't jam or short against anything. You can trim the leads down to about ½".

If your rectifier leads are in a single line, the two end leads are DC, and the two center leads are AC. The positive DC lead, besides being longer, is identifiable by a plus sign and sometimes by a bevel on the corner of the case. If your rectifier leads are arranged in the shape of a square, the positive lead has a similar identifying mark and is diagonally opposite the negative lead.

Mount the engine rectifier. Mount the rectifier so that you can still identify the positive DC lead after the rectifier is in place. Make sure the surfaces are free of oil and dirt, and attach the rectifier with silicone sealant. Let the sealant cure overnight.

Should you decide sometime in the future to sell the engine, you can pull the rectifier off, remove the silicone sealant with a wooden stick, and reinstall the old E-unit.

WIRE THE CIRCUIT BOARD AND MOTOR UNITS

Wire the main circuit board. You will need four pieces of 18 gauge solid wire: two to go from the AC barrier strip to the AC terminals of the rectifier, and two to go from the DC terminals of the rectifier to the DC barrier strip. Each DC wire is also connected to a lead of the filter capacitor. Refer to fig. 6-5 for orientation.

Attach the AC wires. Measure a piece of wire long enough to go from an AC rectifier terminal to the barrier strip, with some slack. Then add about ½" for attaching it to the screw in the terminal.

There are two ways to attach these wires to the rectifier, First, you can use a female disconnect (push on terminal), attaching the wire to the disconnect with the crimping tool. Once the wire is firmly attached, just push it onto the rectifier terminal. Or you can solder one end directly to the AC rectifier terminal. If you solder the wire directly, you will need a large soldering gun, needle-nose pliers for a heatsink, and a rubber band. Tin the wire. Insert it in the hole in the terminal, and wrap it around the terminal once or twice. Squeeze it with the needle-nose pliers to make sure the joint is firm. If you use Radio Shack's 50-PIV rectifier, don't forget to connect the diode to the DC terminals at the same time, cathode (banded end) of the diode to the positive terminal of the rectifier. Clamp the pliers onto the terminal between the joint and the case, using a rubber band around the handles to keep it closed. Then solder the joint. If you are attaching the protection diode, also clamp the small soldering heatsink onto the diode lead, between the solder joint and the

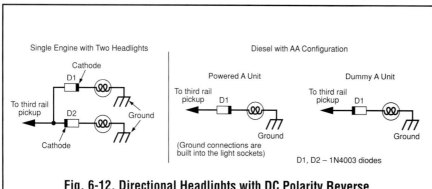

Fig. 6-12. Directional Headlights with DC Polarity Reverse

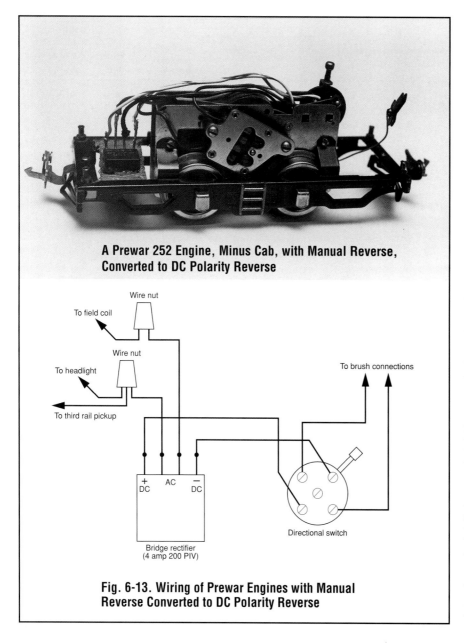

A Prewar 252 Engine, Minus Cab, with Manual Reverse, Converted to DC Polarity Reverse

Fig. 6-13. Wiring of Prewar Engines with Manual Reverse Converted to DC Polarity Reverse

diode. To attach the other end of the wire to the barrier strip, first remove the screw. Wrap the end of the wire around the screw, lower the screw into its hole, and tighten it.

Attach the second wire to its terminal and the barrier strip in the same way as you attached the first one.

Attach the DC wires. As shown in fig. 6-5, these wires are attached to their terminals on the rectifier and the DC barrier strip in the same way as the AC wires. Each wire is also attached to a lead on the filter capacitor. Note that this capacitor is polarized, and each lead has to be connected to the proper wire. Strip a section about ⅜" in the middle of each wire and wind it once around the small paper clip to make a loop. Push the loop onto the appropriate capacitor lead, squeeze it tight, and solder it in place. Repeat the procedure with the other capacitor terminal. Cut off any excess capacitor lead.

Wire the engine rectifier. Use 22 gauge stranded wire. It has enough slack so that the motor can move right and left easily.

Postwar engines with three-position E-units. Engines with three-position E-units (fig. 6-10) have a single field coil winding and only two connections to the field coil. One is usually the ground connection, and the other goes to the lug through which the field coil was connected to the E-unit.

Run one wire from an AC terminal on the rectifier to the field coil lug. Make sure it is long enough to allow the motor to move freely. Strip the ends of the wire. Wind one end of the wire around the large plastic-coated paper clip, forming a loop with two or three turns. Push the loop onto the rectifier terminal until it is about ¼" from the case. Clamp the needle-nose pliers onto the lead between the wire and the case, and solder the wire in place. You may need to use a heavy-duty soldering gun. With the needle-nose pliers, wrap the other end of the wire tightly around the field coil lug and solder lt.

If the connection to the field coil is a splice to another wire, first push a ¾" length of 1/16" or 3/32" heat-shrink tubing onto one wire. Then twist the wires together and solder them. Push the heat-shrink tubing over the soldered joint and shrink it in place with hot air from a hair dryer.

The second wire goes from the other AC rectifier lead to the hot wire connection to the third-rail pickup. While you can solder this wire directly to the rectifier lead, it is easier first to solder a separate wire to the rectifier lead, and then to join this wire to the hot wire with a wire nut.

Lightly sand the wires and twist them together, along with the wires from headlight and smoke generator, if any. Then screw the wire nut onto them. The wire nut simplifies joining all these wires and also makes it easier to install other circuitry later on.

The third and fourth wires each go from a DC rectifier lead to a brush terminal. Connect them to the solder lugs on the brushplate the same way you connected the wire to the field coil lug. But do not solder the wires to the rectifier yet. Make loops in their ends with the large paper clip and just push them onto the rectifier leads, leaving them unsoldered for the time being. If you are using a 50-PIV rectifier, connect a 1N4003 diode between the DC terminals, cathode to positive rectifier terminal or between the corresponding brushplate terminals. Coil the ends of the diode leads just like a wire. If your engine is grounded through one brush connection, one wire goes from the other brush connection to an AC rectifier terminal, and two wires go from the field coil to the DC rectifier terminals.

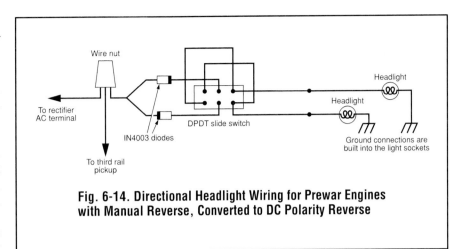

Fig. 6-14. Directional Headlight Wiring for Prewar Engines with Manual Reverse, Converted to DC Polarity Reverse

Postwar engines with two-position E-units, or manual reversing switches. Refer to fig. 6-11. Engines equipped with these devices require a little extra work because of their double-wound field coils. The free end of the field coil winding that you will use must be grounded. If the wire is long enough, you can ground it through one of the brushplate screws. For this purpose, do not use any brushplate screw with a plastic washer attached to it. The washer was originally intended to isolate wires from the ground and will not form a ground connection. Instead switch the brushplate screws, and for the ground connection use the other screw, which lacks the plastic washer. Solder the wire to a terminal lug, and screw it in with the washerless screw. Radio Shack does not sell solder lugs, only what it calls "solderless ring tongues," but you can solder these devices just the same. Just pass the wire through the small end of the lug and wrap it around tight before you solder.

If the wire is not long enough, you will have to splice a piece of 22 gauge stranded wire to the end before connecting it. Solder the wires together, and insulate the joint with heat-shrink tubing. If the wire is too short to splice, you

will have to carefully unwind a piece from the field coil and proceed from there. Whatever you do, make sure that the delicate field coil wire isn't going to get caught in anything as the motor turns. If any wire on the field coil winding is loose, carefully tape it in place.

Once you have modified the field coil connections, you can follow the procedure outlined for motors with three-position E-units.

You can equip all double-ended engines with directional headlights when you install DC polarity reverse. Connect a 1-amp diode in series with each headlight, as shown in fig. 6-12. The 1-amp diodes serve as one way electrical valves, so that the direction of the current flow determines which headlight is lit. As a result it is easy to ensure that only the forward headlight is lit when the engine is moving. If the wrong headlight is lit, switch the diodes. You may, however, wish to postpone this step, and instead install one of the constant-intensity directional headlight circuits described in Chapter 8.

Prewar engines. Nonreversible Engines (for example, 248 and 261), came with neither an E-unit nor a manual reversing switch. Their wiring is straightforward, and they can be converted to DC polarity reverse with relatively little

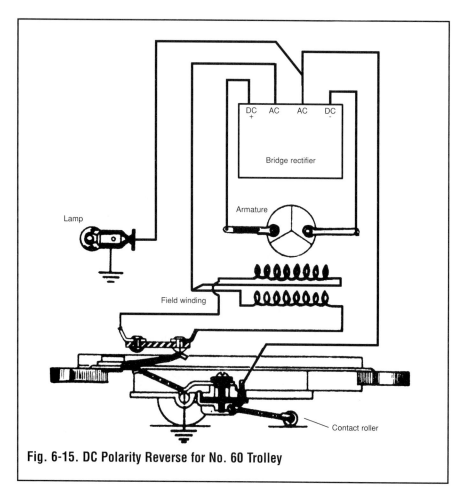

Fig. 6-15. DC Polarity Reverse for No. 60 Trolley

reverse will change the position of the trolley pole.

Refer to fig. 6-15, and proceed as follows: Find the third-rail pickup wire. It is usually black and disappears into the body of the car. Unsolder it from one brushplate lug. Then unsolder the two field coil wires from the other brushplate lug. Work slowly and carefully, because the field coil wires are delicate. Make sure to keep them together. Do not disturb the other two field coil wires, connected to the reversing switch (the plastic rectangle in the middle of the car). Trim the leads on the 4-amp rectifier, and with silicone sealant mount the rectifier vertically on the reversing switch or in another convenient spot. Let the sealant cure overnight.

Next, connect the third-rail pickup wire and the wire from the light to one AC rectifier terminal. You can solder the wires directly to this rectifier terminal. Or you can solder a single wire to the rectifier terminal, and use a wire nut to connect that wire to the third-rail pickup wire and the wire from the light.

Solder the two field coil wires to the other AC rectifier terminal. If the field coil wires are too short, splice a length of wire to them, and insulate the splice with heat-shrink tubing. Now run a wire from each DC rectifier terminal to a brushplate lug, and solder it.

No. 50 gang car. The no. 50 gang car can be modified the same way as the trolley (fig. 6-16). There is, however, considerably less room for the circuit, and it is necessary to wedge the rectifier under the engine hood.

Engines with can motors. Today a growing number of engines are equipped with can motors, permanent magnet DC motors housed in cylindrical cases. Because a DC motor uses lower voltage than a universal motor operating on AC, its electronic E-unit is designed to

trouble. Use the wiring layout in fig. 6-10.

If your engine has manual reverse, you can retain the manual reverse if you so wish. Connect the disk reversing switch between the brush terminals and the DC rectifier leads, as shown in fig. 6-13. The AC rectifier leads are connected to the field coil and third-rail pickup, as usual. If your engine has two headlights, and you wish to add directional lighting, you will also have to install a DPDT switch between the headlight diodes and the headlights (fig. 6-14). Whenever you change directions manually, you will also have to throw the headlight switch. Otherwise, the wrong headlight will be lit. Once you have manually set the headlights, changing the track polarity to reverse the engine will

automatically turn on the correct headlight.

Other prewar engines with E-units, whether the old pendulum units or the more modern three-position devices, can be converted to DC polarity reverse the same way as postwar engines (fig. 6-10).

No. 60 trolley car. If you have a Lionel no. 60 trolley car, you can convert it to DC polarity reverse and still retain the bumper-operated reverse. This is useful if you want to back the car out of an inaccessible piece of trackage and cannot reach the bumper to change directions.

There are two limitations to keep in mind: first, the bumper-operated reverse will work only when it is extended in the direction in which the car is traveling; and, second, only the bumper-operated incorporate voltage reduction. DC operation renders the E-unit unnecessary, and therefore some other way must be found to reduce the voltage. Otherwise the motor will run too fast and might even burn out. The simplest way to reduce the voltage is to use a couple of 4-amp bridge rectifiers (276-1146) wired as voltage droppers, as shown in fig. 6-17. Three or four are usually sufficient.

To wire a rectifier as a voltage dropper, you must connect a diode across its DC terminals. This method is identical to that used in the voltage droppers for the CD unit in Chapter 5, except that it uses 3-amp diodes (276-1141) instead of 1-amp units. Voltage droppers are also used in the constant-intensity lighting circuits discussed in Chapter 8. In fact, you might wish to take advantage of the opportunity to install constant-intensity lighting, as it entails only a little additional wiring.

It is easiest to wire the rectifiers before you mount them. Use the Helping Hands to hold each rectifier still when you work on it, and coil the end of each wire on a large paper clip, as described in Step 8a above. Solder small pieces (about 1½") of 22 gauge stranded wire to each of the DC terminals. Then solder each diode to these wires, cathode (banded end) to negative rectifier terminal. Next, connect the rectifier assemblies to each other by wires to their AC terminals, as shown in fig. 6-17. If you need more voltage reduction, add more rectifiers. Mount the rectifiers with silicone sealant, and use wire nuts to connect them to the motor lead and the third-rail pickup. Make sure the bare leads don't touch each other.

Disconnect the horn or whistle circuit. Because the horn and whistle circuits are triggered by DC, they will sound constantly if you power your engines with DC.

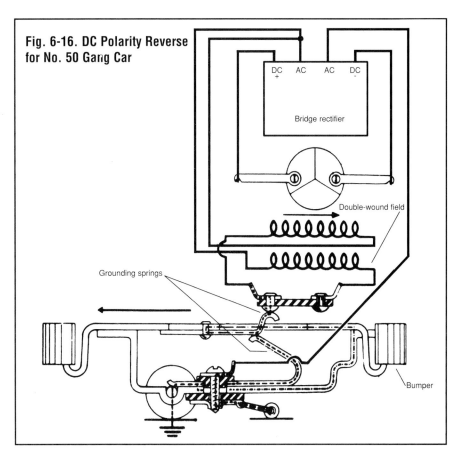

Fig. 6-16. DC Polarity Reverse for No. 50 Gang Car

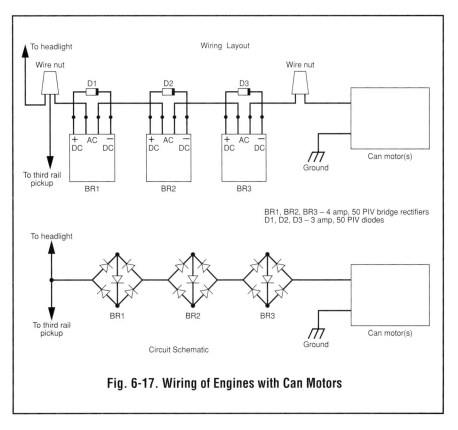

Fig. 6-17. Wiring of Engines with Can Motors

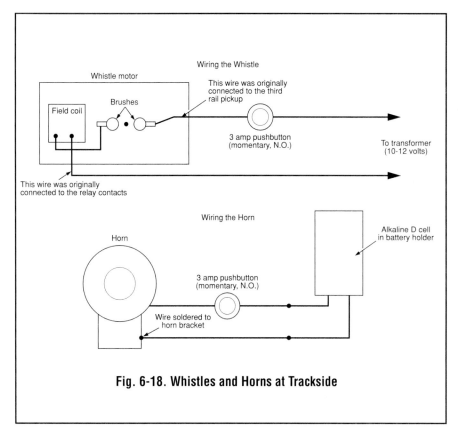

Fig. 6-18. Whistles and Horns at Trackside

Find the connection to the third-rail pickup, unsolder it, and tape the bare wires. You can also simply remove the horn relay, horn, and battery bracket, which are attached by machine screws. Removing these parts together with the E-unit will free up valuable engine space for other uses. Nevertheless, save everything for reinstallation if sometime in the future you decide to sell the engine.

You now have three options:

If you don't care, you can simply do without the horn or whistle.

You can purchase a commercial horn or whistle circuit designed for use with DC track voltage.

You can mount the horn or whistle trackside on its own circuit. Lionel, in fact, once manufactured trackside whistles for operators whose house current was DC or low-frequency AC. Operators of small layouts might find this a satisfactory alternative.

If you mount the whistle trackside (fig. 6-18), power it through the right-hand brush terminal and the field coil wire that was originally attached to the relay contacts. Bypass or remove the relay, and install a 3-amp N.O. (normally open) push button (275-1556). Connect the circuit to its own transformer or to the constant-voltage terminal on your main transformer. Do not change the connection between the other brush terminal and the field coil, or the whistle motor will turn the wrong way. When you mount the whistle, elevate it a little, so that the opening to the bottom air chamber is not blocked.

If you mount the horn trackside (fig. 6-18), solder a wire to the horn bracket, which serves as a ground. Install a battery holder (270-403) and a 3-amp N.O. push button. Use an alkaline D cell. **Do not try to solder any wires directly to the battery, as it could explode.**

If you have a rotating search-light car, you will have to disconnect the coil, which will heat up on DC. Other accessories that use AC, such as the cattle car, must have their own fixed-voltage AC source. They can, however, use the sane ground connection as the DC track circuit.

TEST AND INSTALL THE CIRCUIT

Check all your wiring and solder joints. Make sure that there are no potential short circuits or open connections and that the polarities of the capacitor and diode leads are correct. Connect the AC terminals of the barrier strip to a transformer, and the DC terminals to the track. The terminal connected to the positive rectifier terminal should go to the center rail.

Turn the current on. If the engine moves forward, solder the wires to its DC rectifier terminals. If the engine moves into reverse, switch the wires to the DC rectifier terminals before you solder them. If the engine doesn't move at all, find out what the trouble is and correct it. The problem is usually either a short circuit or an open connection.

If the engine runs too fast at the lowest transformer setting, you have two choices. You can add the throttle discussed in the next chapter. Or you can install one to three voltage droppers in the engine. If you choose the second alternative, read the section above on can motors and voltage droppers. Then refer to fig. 6-19. Use 6-amp rectifiers (276-1181) and 3-amp diodes (276-1141) in postwar motors, which use a lot of current. You can install the voltage droppers between the third-rail pickup wire and its connection to the engine's directional rectifier. Connect the voltage droppers to one another temporarily with wire nuts. Add one voltage dropper at a time, until the speed of the engine is satisfactory. You can then solder the voltage droppers together. Use wire nuts to connect to voltage dropper bank to the rest of the engine circuit, and screw the headlight and smoke generator wires into the same wire nut as the third-rail pickup wire. You can also use voltage droppers to increase the output of smoke generators by raising the track voltage needed to operate at any given speed. If later you decide to install the throttle in the next chapter, you may have to remove one or more voltage droppers in order to increase the engine speed.

Referring to fig. 6-20, remove the wires from the circuit board to the track and connect the DPDT switch. The wires from the center terminals of the switch go to the DC terminals on the circuit board, and the remaining two wires go to the track.

Now try it out. With the DPDT switch, you should be able to control the direction of the engine at will. Once you have determined that everything works you can install the circuit on your layout.

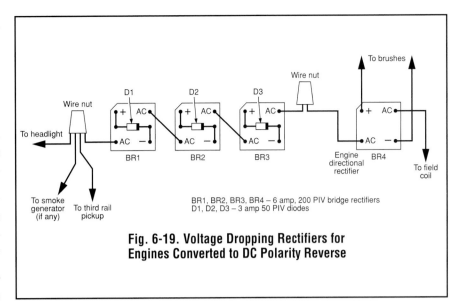

BR1, BR2, BR3, BR4 – 6 amp, 200 PIV bridge rectifiers
D1, D2, D3 – 3 amp 50 PIV diodes

Fig. 6-19. Voltage Dropping Rectifiers for Engines Converted to DC Polarity Reverse

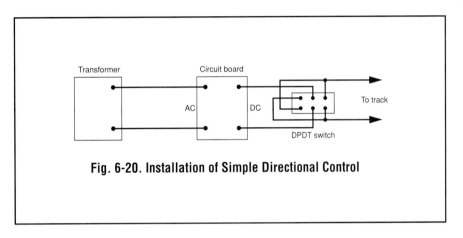

Fig. 6-20. Installation of Simple Directional Control

7

Combination Throttle and Directional Control

This chapter presents a combination throttle and directional control. This circuit (fig. 7-1) is well suited for engines that, after conversion to DC polarity reverse, run too fast at the lowest transformer setting. The circuit also makes possible the use of older transformers, which otherwise would be unsuitable for powering trains.

HOW THE THROTTLE WORKS

The throttle operates as a switch, turning the current on 120 times a second. Alternating current normally starts at zero voltage, rises smoothly to a maximum voltage, and falls back to zero. It then repeats the process, flowing in the opposite direction. Each negative or positive pulse of current is known as an alteration, a pair of alternations forming one complete cycle. The term *hertz* (abbreviated Hz) designates the number of cycles per second, 60 for house current in North America. Varying the point at which the current is switched on during each alternation makes it possible control the speed of the motor.

A three-terminal solid-state device known as a *triac* switches the current on during each alternation. When a momentary control current is applied at one terminal (the *gate*), a much heavier working current flows through two other terminals (main terminal 1 and main terminal 2) and continues to flow even after the momentary current stops. The working current continues to flow, in fact, until it is turned off, which in the case of AC occurs at the end of each alternation.

Varying the point at which the momentary current is applied during each alternation determines the amount of working current passed by the triac and thus the speed of the motor. Known as *phase control,* this technique requires few components, needs little space, and is easy to wire. Besides a triac, the throttle consists only of a pot, two resistors, one or two capacitors, and a trigger switch. Charging the capacitor through the pot determines when during each alternation the trigger switch is turned on. The trigger switch then turns on the triac.

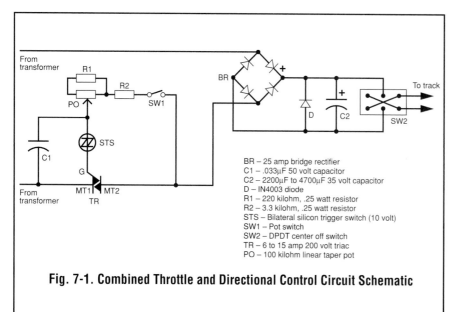

BR – 25 amp bridge rectifier
C1 – .033µF 50 volt capacitor
C2 – 2200µF to 4700µF 35 volt capacitor
D – IN4003 diode
R1 – 220 kilohm, .25 watt resistor
R2 – 3.3 kilohm, .25 watt resistor
STS – Bilateral silicon trigger switch (10 volt)
SW1 – Pot switch
SW2 – DPDT center off switch
TR – 6 to 15 amp 200 volt triac
PO – 100 kilohm linear taper pot

Fig. 7-1. Combined Throttle and Directional Control Circuit Schematic

PARTS, MATERIALS, AND TOOLS

Electronic parts

In addition to the parts specified for the simple DC circuit (Chapter 6), you will need:

.033-µF, 50-volt capacitor (Digi-Key P1018-ND or EF1333-ND; Jameco 26921; Hosfelt 15-416). Or you can use a .01-µF capacitor (272-1065) and a .022-µF capacitor (272-1066) connected in parallel.

6-amp, 400-volt triac (276-1000) per throttle. To power no more than one double-motored postwar engine at a time. If you operate lashups with additional engines, use a larger device, such as Teccor's 15-amp, 200-volt unit (Digi-Key Q2015L5-ND). The larger triac is also advisable if you plan to power the throttle with a large, high-amperage transformer, such as a KW or a ZW. The Teccor triac requires a somewhat higher voltage.

Bilateral silicon trigger switch with a 10-volt switching voltage. This device turns the triac on. Made by Teccor (Digi-Key HS-10-ND).

100-K linear taper pot (271-092).

Pot switch (271-1740)

3.3-K, .25-watt resistor (271-1328). This protects the trigger switch from overload at full throttle.

220-K, .25-watt resistor (271-1350). This reduces the resistance of the pot to about 70 kilohms.

Other parts

One 2-position barrier strip (274-656)

Four-position barrier strip (274-658). Replaces the second two-position barrier strip in the simple directional control.

TO-220 heatsink for the triac. (276-1363)

½" 4-40 machine screw, with nut and lock washer, for mounting the triac. Or use a TO-220 mounting kit (276-1373).

Fuse holder (270-364 or 270-739) and a fast-acting fuse of the appropriate current rating (270-1007, 270-1009, 270-1010, or 270-1011). For details, see the text. Or use the equivalent circuit breaker (Digi-Key PB183-ND, PB184-ND, PB185-ND, or PB186-ND).

Knob for pot assembly (e.g., 274-433)

Materials

Silicone heatsink grease (276-1372)

Silicone rubber sealant (64-2314)

.032 rosin-core solder (64-005)

Plastic tray from a microwave dinner. Medium size, approximately 5" x 6" without separate compartments. The tray must have a PETE 1 logo. Any piece of plastic or wood will work, as long as silicone sealant adheres to it.

Medium-grade sandpaper

Letters and numbers from a videotape label. Radio Shack sells the labels separately (44-1103).

Damp sponge

22 gauge solid wire (278-1215)

18 gauge solid wire (278-1217)

Tools

15- to 30-watt soldering pencil (64-2051, 64-2055, or 64-2067)

100-watt soldering gun (64-2193)

Soldering heatsink (276-1567). Not to be confused with the heatsink on which the triac will be mounted.

Medium-size slotted screwdriver

Small (⅛") slotted screwdriver

Needle-nose pliers (64-1812 or 64-1844)

Flat-nose, or electrician's pliers

Wire stripper/cutter (64-1952 or 64-2129)

Crimping tool (64-404). This tool is optional; see the text.

Small (1¼") straightened paper clip

Large (2") straightened paper clip with plastic coating

Helping Hands (64-2093) or similar project holder

Hobby tool with cutting disks, or hacksaw, for cutting the pot shaft

Safety goggles for use with hobby tool or hacksaw

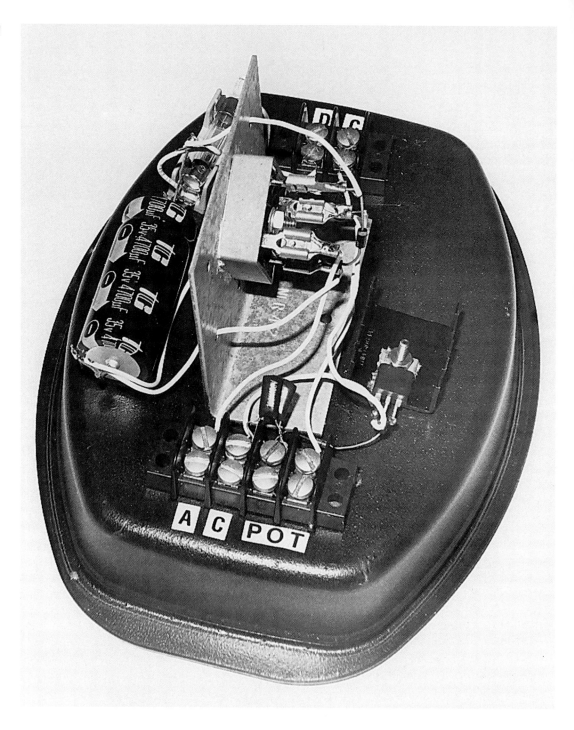

Fig. 7-2. Combined
Directional Control
and Throttle

Current from the triac is rectified by the bridge rectifier and smoothed by the filter capacitor. The end product is a fairly even flow of DC, on which tinplate motors work well. The current now passes through the DPDT switch and then to the track. Motor units equipped with their own rectifiers can now be reversed simply by changing DC polarity with the DPDT switch.

PREPARE AND MOUNT THE PARTS

Mount the triac on the TO-220 heatsink. Mount the triac exactly like the voltage regulator in Chapter 2. Smear a thin coating of silicone heatsink grease (not sealant) on the back of the triac. Place the triac in the TO-220 heatsink over the hole so that its three terminals face you and the hole in the heatsink is away from you. Push the ½" 4-40 machine screw through the back of the heatsink and the triac tab. Install the lock washer and locknut.

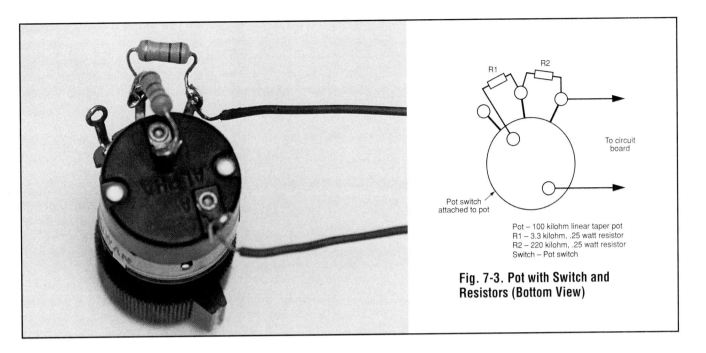

Fig. 7-3. Pot with Switch and Resistors (Bottom View)

R1
R2

To circuit
board

Pot switch
attached to pot

Pot – 100 kilohm linear taper pot
R1 – 3.3 kilohm, .25 watt resistor
R2 – 220 kilohm, .25 watt resistor
Switch – Pot switch

Tighten the locknut and screw with a small screwdriver and pliers.

Now use the pliers to bend each terminal at right angles so that about ¼" sticks up.

Mount the bridge rectifier on its heatsink. Smear a thin coating of heatsink grease on the back of the rectifier, and mount it on the heatsink with the 6-32 machine screw, lock washer, and locknut. If there is no hole in the center of the heatsink, you will have to drill one.

Mount the parts on the back of the microwave dinner tray. Follow the layout in fig. 7-2, and mount the parts with silicone sealant. Do not mount the diode (if needed), the .033-microfarad (or .01-microfarad and .022-microfarad) capacitors, or the trigger switch. Let the sealant cure overnight. Meanwhile, you can work on the pot assembly, the DPDT switch, and the engine rectifier.

Use a hacksaw or hobby tool to trim the pot shaft down to about ½". Don't forget to wear safety goggles.

Install the pot switch on the pot. First turn the shaft of the pot counterclockwise as far as it will go. Then use the small screwdriver to pry up the four tabs that hold the metal cover on, and remove the cover. Push the pot switch on exactly where you removed the cover, making sure that the three solder lugs of the pot are on the same side as the lobes of the switch. The switch should fit precisely, without forcing. Test it by turning the shaft clockwise. It should click and then turn smoothly. If it doesn't, take the switch off, replace the old metal cover (without bending down the tabs), and start over. When you are satisfied that the switch fits, secure it by bending the tabs down with pliers.

Install the resistors on the pot assembly. Refer to fig. 7-3 and clamp the pot upside down in the Helping Hands, so that the three solder lugs point away from you. Connect the 3.3-kilohm resistor to the center solder lug and the nearest lug on the pot switch. Connect the 220-kilohm resistor to the center lug and the right-hand lug. Run the resistor leads through the holes in the solder lugs, and then use the needle-nose pliers to bend

the ends around the lugs so that they are firmly in place. Make sure the bare leads don't touch the metal cover or one another. Don't solder anything yet.

Replace the E-unit in each engine with a rectifier. Follow the procedure for the simple directional control outlined in Chapter 6.

WIRE THE CIRCUIT

Wire the pot assembly. You will need two pieces of 22 gauge solid wire long enough to reach from the location of the pot on your control panel or box to the four-position barrier strip of the main circuit. Refer to fig. 7-3, and attach one wire to the second solder lug on the pot switch, and the other wire to the right-hand lug on the pot. Be certain that no bare wire or resistor lead touches anything metal to which it is not connected.

After you have made sure that the connections are correct and that the joints to the solder lugs are tight, solder the wires and the resistors to their respective lugs.

Install the control knob on the pot shaft. With a small screwdriver, loosen the set screw (in the side of

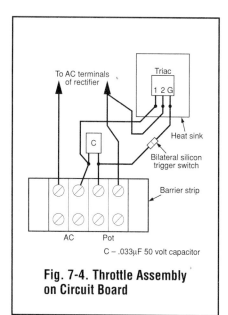

Fig. 7-4. Throttle Assembly on Circuit Board

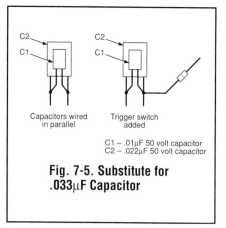

C1 – .01μF 50 volt capacitor
C2 – .022μF 50 volt capacitor

Fig. 7-5. Substitute for .033μF Capacitor

the knob) until the shaft goes all the way in. Then tighten the screw.

Wire the DPDT switch. Follow the procedure for the simple directional control outlined in Chapter 6. Refer to fig. 6-6.

Wire the circuit board. Referring to figs. 7-2 and 7-4, install the throttle circuit between the second AC terminal on the rectifier and one AC terminal on the barrier strip. The components of the circuit consist of: a triac mounted on a heatsink, a silicon trigger switch, and either a single .033-microfarad capacitor or a .01-microfarad capacitor and a .022-microfarad capacitor wired in parallel.

If you use a single .033-microfarad capacitor, connect one lead from the trigger switch to a lead from the capacitor (fig. 7-4). Make sure the other lead is long enough to reach the gate (right-hand terminal) of the triac. Now you will need a piece of 18 gauge wire long enough to connect the second (from left) AC terminal on the barrier strip and main terminal one (left-hand terminal) of the triac: Strip about ½" from each end. Using the small paper clip as a form, make two or three closely

spaced loops in one end. Following fig. 7-4, wrap the capacitor lead to which the trigger switch is not connected around the other end of the 18 gauge wire.

If you use a .022-microfarad capacitor and a .01-microfarad capacitor, begin by connecting them in parallel, as shown in fig. 7-5. Cut the leads of one capacitor to about ¾" and twist them around the leads of the other. Then, connect one lead from the trigger switch to one of the junctions linking the capacitors to each other, as shown in fig. 7-5.

Now you can solder the joints connecting the capacitor or capacitors, the trigger switch, and the wire. Clamp the whole assembly in the Helping Hands and solder each joint. Clamp the soldering heatsink on the lead between the joint and the trigger switch. After you have soldered everything, use the small paper clip to make two or closely spaced loops in the end of the remaining lead from the trigger switch.

Next refer to fig. 7-4, and screw the assembly which you just soldered into the barrier strip. Remove one screw from each of the middle two barrier strip terminals. Wind the capacitor lead around one screw on your right. Then wind the end of the 18 gauge wire around a second screw on your left. Lower the screws into their

holes and tighten them. Next push the other (coiled) end of the 18 gauge wire onto main terminal 1 (left-hand terminal) of the triac. Finally, push the coiled end of the trigger switch lead onto the gate (right-hand terminal) of the triac.

Run an 18 gauge wire from the right-hand terminal of the barrier strip, to one AC terminal of the rectifier and from there to main terminal 2 (center terminal) of the triac. Connect it as follows. Strip 1" from the point in the middle of the wire where it will be attached to the rectifier terminal, and ½" from each end. Make two or three loops in one end with the small paper clip.

First connect the middle section of the wire to the AC rectifier terminal. You can use a crimping tool to attach the wire to a female disconnect and then push the disconnect onto the terminal. Or you can solder it. If you solder the joint, first bend the middle section and insert it in the hole in the terminal. Anchor it, and squeeze it firmly in place with needle-nose pliers. Then solder the connection, using the needle-nose pliers as a heatsink.

Next, remove the screw from the right-hand terminal in the barrier strip, and wind the uncoiled end of the wire around the screw. Then screw everything tight.

Finally push the coiled end of the wire onto main terminal 2 (center terminal) of the triac.

Clamp the soldering heatsink to the triac terminals, and solder all three connections to the triac.

The connections to the remaining AC terminal and the DC terminals of the rectifier are identical to those in the simple directional control. One wire goes from the AC rectifier terminal to the left-hand terminal of the four-terminal barrier strip, and two go from the DC rectifier terminals to terminals on the DC (two-terminal) barrier strip, with connections to the filter capacitor and, if needed, to the fuse holder or circuit breaker (fig. 7-2).

If your transformer does not have its own circuit breaker, install a fuse holder and a fuse, as shown in fig. 7-2. The power rating of the transformer determines the size of the fuse. Transformers up to 45 watts should use a 2- or 2½-amp fast-acting fuse (270-1007 or 270-1008). Transformers from 50 to 75 watts should use a 3- or 4-amp fuse (270-1009 or 270-1010), while those from 75 to 100 watts require a 4- or 5-amp unit (270-1010 or 270-1011). If more than one transformer powers a single throttle, the total wattage of the all transformers determines the size of the fuse. But regardless of total wattage, the fuse should not normally exceed 5 amps.

Instead of one of these fuses, you can use a circuit breaker with a similar current rating. Digi-Key offers Potter and Bromfield breakers rated at 2 amps (PB183-ND), 3 amps (PB184-ND), 4 amps (PB-185-ND), and 5 amps (PB186-ND).

If you use a ZW, KW, or similar large transformer, install a 5-amp fast-acting fuse or circuit breaker, even though the transformer has a circuit breaker of its own. A transformer's circuit breaker is designed to protect the transformer, not other devices. Because these transformers can pass over 10 amps, a short circuit can destroy the triac, which is rated for 6 amps, before it triggers the transformer's circuit breaker. In addition to a separate fuse or breaker, it is also a good idea to install a 15-amp triac with these transformers, as noted in the parts list.

Follow the general procedure for the simple directional control outlined in Chapter 6. If you use Radio Shack's 25-amp, 50-PIV rectifier, install a 1N4003 diode between the DC rectifier terminals, cathode to

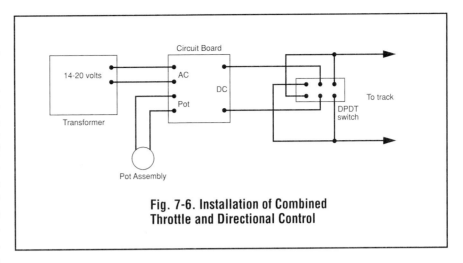

Fig. 7-6. Installation of Combined Throttle and Directional Control

positive rectifier terminal. If you install a fuse holder, connect the wire from a DC rectifier terminal to one solder lug in the fuse holder. Then connect a wire from the other solder lug to a terminal in the DC barrier strip. Install a circuit breaker in the same way.

TEST AND INSTALL THE CIRCUIT

Check the wiring to make sure that all polarities and connections are correct and that no bare joints or wires touch each other. Refer to fig. 7-6 when you test and install the circuit. Connect the wires from the pot assembly to their respective terminals (the two on the right), and the terminals of the DC barrier strip to the track, positive terminal to the center rail.

Then connect the AC barrier strip terminals (the two on the left) to a transformer supplying 14 to 16 volts (18 to 20 volts for a double-motor engine). Turn the pot switch on, and turn the control clockwise. The engine should gradually speed up in the forward direction.

If it runs too fast at the lowest pot setting, reduce the transformer voltage until it just barely moves. If the engine starts fast and then slows as you turn the pot knob, the connections to the two main

terminals on the triac are probably crossed, and you will have to unsolder the wires and switch them. If the engine goes into reverse, switch the connections to the DC leads on the engine rectifier. Once everything is working properly, you can solder the engine rectifier connections.

Now connect the DPDT switch. Replace the wires connected to the DC barrier strip terminals with the DPDT switch wires. The two wires from the center terminals of the switch go to the barrier strip, and the two wires go from the end terminals go to the track.

Finally, try everything out. The pot, with its 270 degree shaft rotation, should provide smooth, gradual acceleration, and the DPDT switch should allow you to control the engine's direction at will. Once you are satisfied that everything works, you can install it permanently on your layout.

ADDING A THROTTLE TO THE SIMPLE DIRECTIONAL CONTROL

If you have already constructed the simple directional control, you can add the throttle to it. On a separate sheet of plastic, construct the throttle assembly, as shown in fig. 7-7. Follow the applicable instructions above, skipping those steps

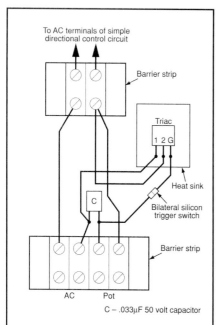

To AC terminals of simple
directional control circuit

Barrier strip

Triac

1 2 G

Heat sink

Bilateral silicon
trigger switch

C

Barrier strip

AC   Pot

C – .033µF 50 volt capacitor

Fig. 7-7. Throttle Assembly for Installation with Simple Directional Control

that deal with the bridge rectifier and the filter capacitor. The throttle circuit board consists only of the triac mounted on its heatsink, the trigger switch, one or two capacitors, a two-position barrier strip, and a four-position barrier strip. Because this circuit carries full track power, use no. 18 gauge wire.

To install the throttle, follow fig. 7-8. Connect the pot and the transformer to their respective terminals on the four-position barrier strip of the throttle circuit. Then connect the two-position barrier strip of the throttle assembly to the AC terminals of the simple directional control. Finally, connect the DC terminals of the directional control circuit to the DPDT switch, and the DPDT switch to the track.

APPLICATIONS AND POSSIBILITIES

The combined throttle and directional control makes available two additional sources of train power: prewar transformers and postwar O27 starter set transformers.

It is easy to purchase prewar transformers at most train meets, often at lower cost than more modern units. Even without circuit breakers, many of these transformers have weathered the decades quite well. However, the lack of smoothly variable speed controls has reduced their desirability and relegated them to fixed-voltage applications, such as powering lights and switches. The combined throttle and directional control makes these transformers much more suitable for powering trains.

Starter set transformers are also inexpensive and readily available at train meets. Lionel sold huge numbers of O27 starter sets, which were equipped with these transformers, ranging in power from 25 to 60 watts. These units are far more common than Lionel's larger and more expensive transformers, which were sold separately, usually to power O gauge sets.

Ray Plummer recognized that several small transformers could provide as much power as a single large one at a fraction of the cost. He suggested dividing a layout into separate blocks and powering each block with one transformer. To do this, it is necessary to use a common ground and to phase the transformers (that is, to connect them so that their voltage alternations coincide), in order to avoid short circuits as trains pass between blocks.

This scheme can be adapted to the combined throttle and directional control. Each transformer can power its own individual circuit. Or two or three transformers can supply a single circuit with enough amperage to power a double-motored engine and passenger cars (fig. 7-9). Prewar as well as postwar transformers are suitable for this application. In fact, both types can power the same throttle, as long as their voltages are the same.

In either case, you must phase the transformers. Arrange the transformers in a row, and plug them in. If you are using small postwar O27 transformers with two binding posts, proceed as follows: Connect a wire between the left-hand terminal of one transformer and the left-hand terminal of a second transformer. Adjust the speed controls so that voltages are approximately the same. Then connect a wire to the right-hand terminal of the first transformer, and touch it to the right-hand terminal of the second transformer. If nothing happens, the transformers are phased. If you get a spark, reverse the plug of one transformer. Repeat the procedure with any additional

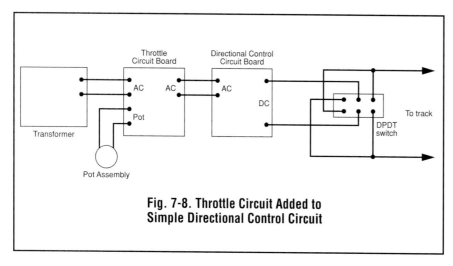

Throttle
Circuit Board

Directional Control
Circuit Board

AC   AC   AC

DC

Pot

To track

DPDT
switch

Transformer

Pot Assembly

Fig. 7-8. Throttle Circuit Added to Simple Directional Control Circuit

transformers. If you are using pre-war transformers, use the 16-volt binding posts and follow the same procedure. Ray Plummer also suggests plugging the transformers into an outlet strip, so that you won't have to phase them again.

Individually powered throttles permit a more rational and flexible system of wiring. Additional small and medium-size transformers can power lights and accessories independently of the throttle circuits, without affecting track voltage. Such independently powered circuits can usually share a common ground with the throttle circuits, simplifying wiring and making troubleshooting easier.

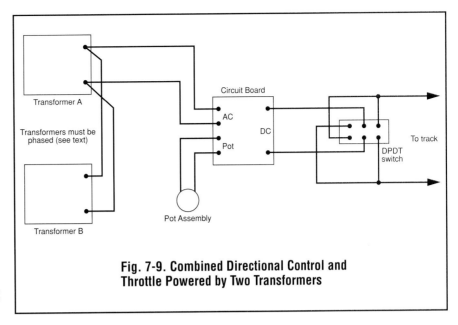

Fig. 7-9. Combined Directional Control and Throttle Powered by Two Transformers

8

Constant-Intensity Lighting Circuits

CONSTANT-INTENSITY LIGHTING FOR MOST TINPLATE LOCOMOTIVES

For over thirty years, scale modelers have used solid-state circuits to provide constant-intensity lighting for their engines and cars. With a few modifications, tinplaters can do the same for theirs.

HOW CONSTANT-INTENSITY LIGHTING WORKS

Current passing through a silicon diode drops a constant .6 volt, regardless of the voltage applied. Circuits in Chapters 5 and 6 made use of this fact, and this chapter offers an additional application.

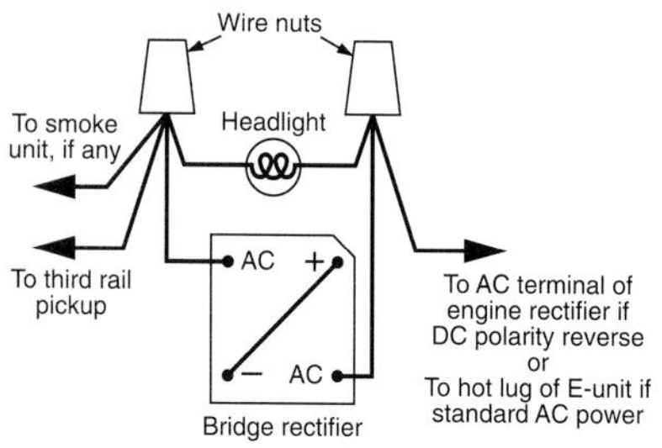

Fig. 8-1. Nondirectional Constant Intensity Lighting (Engine with Universal Motors)

Connecting two diodes in series, anode to cathode, doubles the voltage drop to 1.2 volts. This voltage drop represents lost energy, which can be recovered by connecting a 1.5-volt bulb across the end terminals of the diode assembly. Since the voltage drop is constant, so is the brightness of the light emitted. To insure that the circuit will operate regardless of current polarity, a second pair of diodes, facing in the opposite direction, is usually added.

The entire assembly is connected in series with the motor. Therefore, the diodes must be large enough carry the full motor current. For this reason, lighting circuits for HO locomotives are usually unsuitable for tinplate use. Tinplate locomotives use more current and thus require larger diodes.

A postwar motor uses about 1.5 amps. Thus, a two-motor F3 or GG1 uses a hefty 3 amps. The can motors in more recent locomotives use somewhat less. However, to play it safe, the circuits outlined here assume that our motors are postwar energy guzzlers. To be absolutely safe, diodes should have current ratings at least twice

that of the motors they are intended for. This means at least 3 amps per motor. Six-amp diodes, therefore, are specified for double motor GG1s and F3s.

While you can construct the lighting circuit from separate diodes, it is easier to use a bridge rectifier. A bridge rectifier is simply a network of four diodes. By connecting the DC terminals to each other, you can convert it to a voltage dropper, which supplies constant voltage to the headlights. (The rectifier circuits in this chapter are modified from a circuit published by Peter Thorne in *34 New Electronic Projects for Model Railroaders,* originally intended for HO and N gauge equipment.)

As a voltage dropper, a bridge rectifier has only half the current rating it has when used as an ordinary AC to DC rectifier. Thus a single motor engine, which requires a 3-amp voltage dropper, needs a 6-amp rectifier, and a double-motor engine needs a 12-amp unit. Although Radio Shack does not currently sell a 12-amp rectifier, its 25-amp rectifier (276-1185) should work, provided there is room for it.

Figure 8-1 shows a bridge rectifier wired for constant-intensity lighting. A jumper wire connects the DC terminals, while the wires to the motor, the third-rail pickup, and the headlight are connected to the AC terminals.

For most engines, a single 1.5-volt mini lamp (1272-1139) is satisfactory. Engines with dual headlights can use two mini lamps mounted together and connected in parallel (See Figure 8-6). Owners of engines with lighted number boards and marker lamps might prefer the larger no. 14 bulb. Rated for 300 milliamps at 2.47 volts, it uses about 150 milliamps at 1.2 volts and is well suited for postwar engines or modern engines with universal motors. A few modern engines with can motors may not draw enough current (at least .2 amps) to light the no. 14 bulb. In addition, since this bulb takes a larger E-10 screw base (272-356), finding room for it may present a problem. In two-motor engines wired for AC, with an E-unit, a horn, and motors, it may be difficult to find a place for the circuit and the light.

The nondirectional lighting circuit described below will work on both AC and DC. The directional circuit will work only on locomotives equipped with DC polarity reverse and on AC locomotives equipped with can motors and electronic E-units.

PREPARE AND MOUNT THE PARTS

Prepare the rectifiers and diodes. For each engine, take a little time to plan the circuit layout. Place the rectifier where it will not jam, short out against anything metal, or interfere with the movement of the motor. Make sure there is room to wire the circuit so that nothing will get tangled in moving parts. Finally, try to leave some space for future electronic circuits.

PARTS, MATERIALS, AND TOOLS

Parts and materials
1.5-volt, 25-mA mini lamp (272-1139). Up to four for each locomotive. For more light, use a no. 14 bulb (272-1132) and a compact E-10 socket (272-356), if it will fit. See the discussion in the text.
Bridge rectifier for each motor unit. Single-motor engines and engines with two truck-mounted can motors can use a 6- to 8-amp unit (276-1181). Double-motor engines and engines with large frame-mounted can motors can use a rectifier 12 amps or larger. Radio Shack's 25-amp, 50-PIV rectifier (276-1185) is satisfactory, although there may be a problem finding room for it. For directional lighting, the next item is also necessary.
3-amp or 6-amp, 50-PIV diode, one for each motor unit if you plan to install directional lighting. 6-amp rectifiers require the 3-amp diode (276-1141), while rectifiers 12 amps or larger require the 6-amp unit (276-1661).
Two IN4001 diodes per motor unit (276-1101). For directional lighting.
22 gauge stranded wire (278-1218)
Silicone sealant (64-2314)
Plastic tray from a microwave dinner, not divided into compartments
1/16" or 1/8" heat-shrink tubing (278-1627)
Wire nuts (64-3057), two to five per engine, depending on the circuit
Medium-grade sandpaper
032" rosin-core solder (64-005)
Flashlight battery.

Tools
15- to 30-watt soldering pencil (64-2051 or 64-2055)
50- to 100-watt soldering iron or gun (64-2193)
Push pin
Awl or reamer
Needle-nose pliers (64-1844)
Small (1¼") straightened paper clip
Large (2") straightened plastic-coated paper clip
Wire stripper/cutter (64-1952)
Wide rubber band
Utility knife
Scissors
Helping Hands project holder (64-2093)

Single-bulb or nondirectional lighting. Wire the rectifier. Clamp the rectifier in the Helping Hands and trim its leads to about ⅜". Next cut a piece of wire about 2" long. Strip ½" from each end, and sand the ends until they are bright. Wind each end around the large paper clip, forming two or three tight loops. Lightly sand the rectifier leads. Then push each end onto a DC rectifier terminal, leaving about ⅛" between the wire and the case. Clamp the needle-nose pliers between the wire and the case as a heatsink, holding the handles closed with the wide rubber band. Then solder each joint.

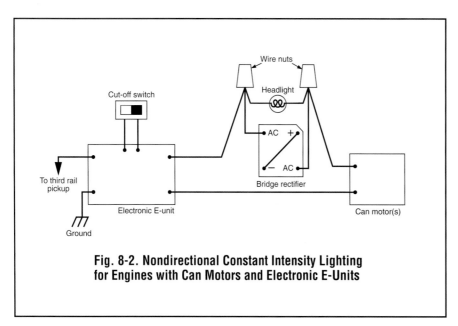

Fig. 8-2. Nondirectional Constant Intensity Lighting for Engines with Can Motors and Electronic E-Units

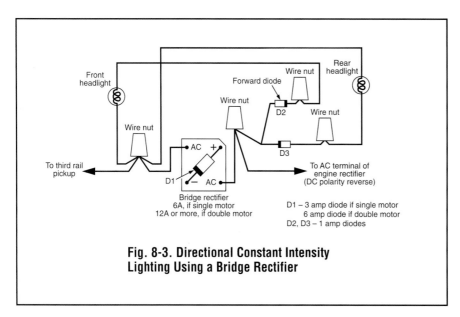

Fig. 8-3. Directional Constant Intensity Lighting Using a Bridge Rectifier

Next, solder a 4" wire to one of the AC terminals. Strip ½" from each end of this wire. Coil one end with the large paper clip, and solder the wire to the AC terminal. Attach a similar wire to the other AC terminal.

Mount the rectifier on the engine frame with silicone sealant, and let the sealant cure overnight.

Prepare the engine. If you use AC and your engine has an old-style electromechanical E-unit, unsol-der the third-rail pickup wire from its lug on the E-unit, and solder a 4" piece of wire to the lug instead. Very likely, two additional wires are soldered to this lug: one for the headlight, and one for the smoke generator, if your engine has one. Unsolder these wires also.

Engines with can motors and electronic E-units can be equipped with constant-intensity lighting (see fig. 8-2). If a wire nut connects the motor or motors to the E-unit,

you can install the lighting circuit at that junction. Remove the wire nut and untwist the wires. You can reuse the old wire nut later when you connect the lighting circuit. If there is no wire nut, you will have to cut the wire and strip the ends first. Engines with can motors and electronic E-units can also use the directional constant-intensity lighting circuit described later.

If you have converted your engine to DC polarity reverse, find the wire nut that joins the hot wire from the third-rail pickup to the wire from an AC rectifier terminal. Remove the wire nut and untwist the wires. Now skip down to the section titled "Prepare and mount the headlights."

Directional lighting. Before you begin, make sure that your engine either is equipped with can motors and an electronic E-unit or has been converted to DC polarity reverse. Otherwise, the directional lighting circuit will not work.

As figs. 8-3 and 8-4 show, the directional lighting circuit requires three additional components besides the rectifier: two 1-amp directional diodes (one for each headlight), and a 3-amp or 6-amp diode (for single- or double-motor engines, respectively). Each 1-amp diode acts like a one-way valve, powering only the forward headlight. But each 1-amp diode also drops the voltage to the headlight .6 volt. Consequently, an additional diode is necessary in the main power circuit in order to replace the lost headlight voltage.
❏ Wire the rectifier and its diode. Attach the power diode to the DC terminals of the rectifier, as shown in fig. 8-3. Trim the diode leads to about ¼" each. Then strip the ends of two 1¼" pieces of 22 gauge stranded wire and coil them with the large paper clip. Clamp the diode in the Helping Hands. Push one end of one wire onto a diode lead and, after attaching the

soldering heatsink (or needle-nose pliers), solder it about ⅛" from the case. Then solder the other wire to the other diode lead. Next, clamp the rectifier in the Helping Hands, and solder each wire to the proper rectifier terminal. The wire from the cathode (the banded end of the diode) goes to the negative rectifier terminal, while the wire from the anode goes to the positive rectifier terminal. If you are using a 25-amp rectifier and a 6-amp diode, you can also attach the diode leads to two female disconnects with a crimping tool and then push the disconnects onto the rectifier terminals. Then solder a 4" piece of 22 gauge wire to each of the AC leads.

❏ Mount the rectifier on the engine frame with silicone sealant, and let the sealant cure overnight.

❏ Wire the directional diode assembly. Line up the 1-amp directional diodes parallel to each other, cathodes (banded ends) facing in opposite directions. Trim the cathode lead of one diode to about 1". With the small paper clip, make two or three loops in the end of this lead, and slide it onto the anode lead of the other diode until it is about ¼" from the case.

Squeeze the joint with needle-nose pliers. Then clamp the two diodes in the Helping Hands, attach the soldering heatsink, and solder the joint.

Solder a 2" piece of wire to the joined leads. Strip ½" from the ends, coil the wire, push it onto the diode lead, and solder it next to the first solder joint. Remove any excess lead. Push a ¾" piece of ⅛" heat-shrink tubing over the joint and lead, and shrink it in place with a hair dryer.

Following the same procedure, attach a 2" piece of wire to each of the other diode leads. Put the completed diode assembly aside.

❏ Prepare the engine. Follow the procedures outlined above.

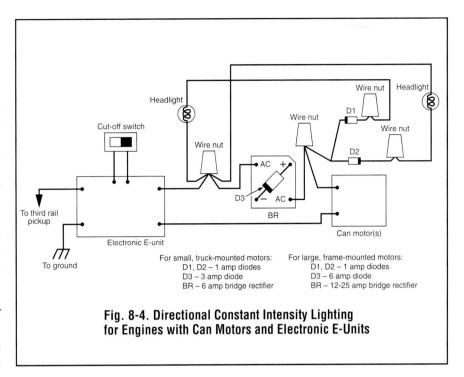

Fig. 8-4. Directional Constant Intensity Lighting for Engines with Can Motors and Electronic E-Units

PREPARE AND MOUNT THE HEADLIGHTS

Wire the headlight bulbs or sockets. It is easiest to wire and mount the bulbs first and connect them to the circuit afterwards.

You will have to consider what kind of bulb to use and where to mount it. The space available will determine whether you can use the mini lamp or the larger no. 14 bulb and socket. In many postwar diesels, the original headlight socket is an integral part of the frame. Since constant-intensity headlights must be insulated from the ground, you cannot use the old socket. You will have to work around it with little room to spare. Steam engines, especially those with smoke generators, often have little clearance. The mounting procedures described below are for your general guidance, and you will have to tailor them to fit the requirements of each engine.

The size of the engine may also limit your choices in headlight illumination. A few engines powered by small can motors draw too

little current to power the no. 14 bulb. In such cases, you will only be able to use the mini lamp. Fortunately, most engines use more current, giving you a choice.

As the diagrams show, wire nuts connect the headlights to wires from the circuit assembly. For each headlight, measure enough wire to go from the headlight location to the wire nut junction. If you are using mini lamps, take their 2" leads into account. If you are installing the directional lighting circuit, note that a wire nut connects each headlight to a 1-amp diode in the two-diode assembly. A third wire nut connects this assembly to a wire from an AC rectifier terminal. (See fig. 8-3.)

Attach the wires to the headlight. If you are using a mini lamp, proceed as follows. Strip ½" from each end of one wire, and use the small paper clip to make two or three closely spaced loops in one stripped end. Push the loops onto a lead from the bulb, squeeze them, and solder the joint. Slide a ¾" length of ⅟₁₆" heat-shrink tubing

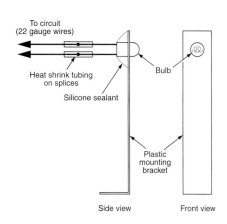

Fig. 8-5. Installation of Headlight, Using a Mini-lamp

over the joint and, with hot air from a hair dryer, shrink it in place. Repeat the procedure with the other wire and lead.

If you are using a no. 14 screw-base bulb and the compact socket, then solder the wires directly to the two solder lugs in the bottom of the socket.

Mount the headlight bulbs on their plastic brackets. First, remove the old headlight bulb and its socket, if possible. Then measure the distance from the center of the headlight lens to the engine frame or to the original headlight mounting bracket. This is especially important if you are using a mini lamp, which must be as close to the headlight lens as possible. Location is not as critical with the no. 14 bulb assembly, which illuminates the entire front end of the engine.

Next, from a microwave dinner tray, cut a strip of plastic about 1½" longer than the distance you just measured and about ¾" wide. Bend the bottom ½" or ¾", so that it forms a mounting flange, as shown in fig. 8-5.

If you are using a mini lamp, make a hole in the plastic strip with the push pin. Center this hole near the top of the strip, locating it the same distance from the bend as the center of the headlight lens is from the engine frame or from the old headlight mounting bracket, if any. Next, push an awl through the hole in the direction the mini lamp will face, and enlarge the hole to accommodate the bulb.

Insert the light bulb into its hole, and secure it from behind with silicone sealant. Let the sealant cure overnight.

For engines with dual headlights, you can use the preceding procedure to mount two mini lamps together on the plastic strip. See fig. 8-6.

If you are using a no. 14 bulb and a compact socket, cut out a T-shaped piece of plastic, with arms about ½" wide. Make the horizontal segment of the T about 1½" long. Adjust the length of the vertical segment to fit the engine. Bend the T at the junction of the two segments. Then, with silicone sealant, mount the socket on the vertical segment, as shown in fig. 8-7.

Mount the headlight assembly in the engine. At this point, make

sure that the headlight assembly has enough clearance at the top when you put on the cab. In some diesels, the headlight lens is at the very top of the cab, and you may have to trim the headlight bracket to get everything to fit. If you are using a mini lamp, locate it right up against the headlight lens.

Extend the headlight wires out through the bottom of the engine, and mount the headlight assembly with silicone sealant. It is sometimes difficult to see whether the headlight assembly is located properly. To ensure that it is, put the cab on the engine, and touch the headlight wires to the terminals of a 1.5-volt flashlight battery. If you get a good light through the headlight lens, you can let the silicone sealant cure. If not, adjust the position of the headlight assembly until it is correct. Mount the rear headlight, if any, the same way.

Connect the wires with wire nuts. When the sealant has cured, push the headlight wires back through the bottom of the engine and connect them to the circuit. Select the appropriate diagram from figs. 8-1 through 8-4, and

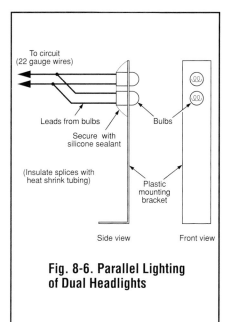

Fig. 8-6. Parallel Lighting of Dual Headlights

To circuit
(22 gauge wires)

Leads from bulbs

Secure with
silicone sealant

(Insulate splices with
heat shrink tubing)

Bulbs

Plastic
mounting
bracket

Side view

Front view

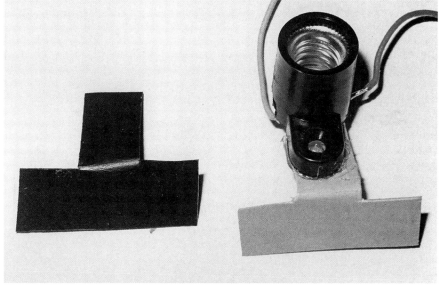

Fig. 8-7. A Compact E-10 Base with Mounting Brackets

connect the wires accordingly. The wire from the smoke generator or the horn relay goes to the same wire nut as the third-rail pickup. Don't forget the two 1-amp diodes if you are installing a directional circuit. Sand the ends of the wires lightly. For each connection, twist the wires together clockwise, and then screw the wire nuts over them until tight. The wire nuts should cover all bare wire.

Test the engine and adjust the connections if necessary. The brightness of the headlight should not vary too much as you increase the voltage. If you have installed a directional lighting circuit, make sure that the headlight is lit in the forward direction when the engine moves. If the wrong headlight is on, switch the wires from the headlights to the 1-amp diodes.

The diode voltage drop (1.2 or 1.8 volts, depending on the circuit), makes a slightly higher transformer voltage necessary to power the engine. Higher voltage, however, has its benefits: it cuts through dirt on the track a little more easily, reducing current interruptions; and it increases the output of smoke generators as well.

At very low voltages, the lights may flicker because the filter capacitor in the throttle is behaving like an oscillator. To cure this problem, you can substitute a smaller capacitor, for example, a 1500-microfarad capacitor for a 2200-microfarad unit. A smaller capacitor will speed up the flicker to the point that you won't be able to see it. Or you can add one or more voltage droppers to the engine motor circuit, which will have the same effect by requiring higher throttle voltage to operate the train.

CONSTANT-INTENSITY LIGHTING FOR AA DIESELS

A little additional work can provide AA diesels with constant-intensity directional lighting. The power unit requires a circuit similar to that shown fig. 8-3, but with only one headlight and one directional diode. This diode, which lights the headlight in the forward direction, is labeled D2 in fig. 8-3.

The dummy engine requires a different approach, as shown in fig. 8-8. The diode in this circuit powers the headlight only when the dummy engine moves forward. The filter capacitor and voltage regulator smooth out the current and keep it at 5 volts. A 6.3-volt, .15-amp bulb with bayonet base or a 6-volt, 25-milliamp mini lamp is the light source.

CONSTRUCT THE CIRCUIT

Cut out the circuit board. From the microwave dinner tray, cut out a plastic rectangle about 1¼" x 2". Score it with a utility knife, and then cut it with scissors.

Mount the parts on the circuit board. Begin by assembling the voltage regulator and its heatsink. Smear a thin coating of silicone heatsink grease (not sealant) on the back of the voltage regulator. Place the voltage regulator in the heatsink over the hole so that its three terminals face you. Push the ½" 4-40 machine screw through the back of the heatsink and the voltage regulator tab. Install the lock washer and locknut. Tighten the locknut and screw with a small screwdriver and pliers. Now use the pliers to bend the three terminals about ¼" from the ends at right angles, so that they face up.

Next, mount all the parts except the diode on the plastic rectangle with silicone sealant (see fig. 8-9).

PARTS, MATERIALS, AND TOOLS

Electronic parts

1-amp diode (276-1101), for the dummy engine
220-µF, 35-volt electrolytic capacitor with radial leads (272-1029)
1.4-amp bridge rectifier (276-1152), for number boards in the dummy engine or for cars
7805 voltage regulator (276-1770)
No. 47 bulb (272-1110) and bayonet-base socket (272-355). A no. 1847 bulb (272-1115) will also work, but it uses three times as much current. Instead of these bulbs and the socket, you can use the 6-volt, 25-mA mini lamp (272-1140). In some engines, the mini lamp will light the headlight, but not the number board lights.
TO-220 heatsink (276-1363)

Other parts

22 gauge stranded wire (278-1218)
Plastic tray from a microwave dinner, preferably one not divided into compartments
.032" rosin-core solder (64-005)
Medium-grade sandpaper
Silicone heatsink grease (276-1372)
Silicone sealant (64-2314)
½" 4-40 machine screw with lock washer and nut, or use a TO-220 mounting kit (276-1373)

Tools

15- to 30-watt soldering pencil/iron (64-2051 or 64-2055)
40- to 100-watt soldering gun, if needed (64-2193)
Soldering heatsink (276-1567). Not to be confused with the heatsink on which the voltage regulator will be mounted.
Small (⅛") slotted screwdriver
Needle-nose pliers (64-1812 or 64-1844)
Wire stripper/cutter (64-1952)
Small (1.25") paper clip
Helping Hands (64-2093) or similar project holder
Utility knife
Scissors

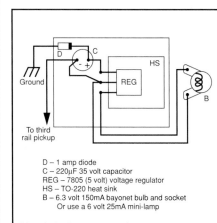

D – 1 amp diode
C – 220µF 35 volt capacitor
REG – 7805 (5 volt) voltage regulator
HS – TO-220 heat sink
B – 6.3 volt 150mA bayonet bulb and socket
Or use a 6 volt 25mA mini-lamp

Fig. 8-8. Directional Constant intensity Lighting – Nonpowered Engine Unit

After the sealant has cured overnight, you can wire the circuit.

Wire the circuit board. For each connection, strip ½" from each end of the wire, and lightly sand it. Wind two or three turns of one end tightly around the paper clip. Trim the excess, and with needle-nose pliers, press the turns close together. Remove the wire from the paper clip, and push it onto the component lead until it is about ⅛" from the case. Squeeze the joint tight. Attach the soldering heatsink between the joint and the case, and solder the joint.

Wire the circuit board as follows:
❏ Solder the cathode lead of the diode directly to the positive lead of the capacitor, but be sure to leave enough of the capacitor lead for the next step.

❏ From the positive lead of the capacitor, run a wire to the input (left-hand) terminal of the voltage regulator, and solder it.

❏ From the negative lead of the capacitor run a wire to the center terminal of the voltage regulator, and then to a solder lug on the light socket. Leave about ⅜" of capacitor lead for another joint. To connect this wire to the voltage regulator, strip about ⅜" from the center of the wire. Coil the stripped section with the small paper clip, push it onto the regulator terminal, squeeze it tight, and solder it.

❏ Attach one 5" wire to the anode lead of the diode, and one to the negative capacitor lead. These will go to the ground and to the third-rail pickup, respectively.

❏ Run a wire from the output (right-hand) terminal of the voltage regulator to the other solder lug on the light socket, and solder it.

❏ Check all the connections to make sure that the joints are strong and that no bare wires or leads touch each other or the heatsink. Trim any excess pieces of leads.

Fig. 8-9. Unwired Directional Lighting Circuit for Dummy Engine

Mount the light socket on its bracket. Cut out a bracket from a microwave dinner tray. Punch a hole in the center to accommodate the center contact of the socket, which protrudes when the bulb is inserted. Mount the light socket on the bracket with silicone sealant. Be careful not to get sealant on the center contact.

Mount the circuit board together with the light socket and its bracket in the dummy engine. Be sure that the socket and its solder lugs are isolated from the ground—that is, that they do not touch any metal part of the engine.

Make the final connections

❏ Connect the wire from the anode lead of the diode to the ground. Most of the time, you can solder or screw this wire to the engine frame. If, however, the engine frame is not part of the ground, look for a ground wire. The ground wire is usually connected to copper strips that rub against the axles in one truck. You can use a wire nut for this connection.

❏ Use a wire nut to connect the wire from the negative capacitor terminal to the wire from the third-rail pickup.

TEST THE CIRCUIT

To test the circuit, put the powered engine and the dummy engine on the track. When the powered unit moves backwards, its headlight should be off and that of the dummy unit should be on. The brightness of the light should not vary much as the voltage is increased. If the headlight of the dummy engine is lit when the powered unit moves forward, reverse the connections to the ground and the third-rail pickup in the dummy engine. If the headlight of the powered unit is lit when the powered unit moves in reverse, reverse the 1-amp diode connected to the headlight.

CONSTANT-INTENSITY LIGHTING FOR CARS

With a single modification, the circuit in fig. 8-10 can furnish constant-intensity lighting for cars. In place of the 1-amp diode, use a 1.4-amp bridge rectifier, as shown. To furnish more light for larger cars, you can add a second bulb and socket in parallel with the first, provided both bulbs are low current no. 47 units. Once again, make sure that the connections to the light socket are isolated from the ground.

To accommodate the protruding center contact of the light socket, first mount a ¼" length of soda straw on the plastic rectangle. Then mount the light socket on the straw.

WIRE THE CIRCUIT

Connect the wires as follows:

❏ From one rectifier to the third-rail pickup.

❏ From the other AC rectifier terminal to the ground.

❏ From the positive (+) DC rectifier terminal to the positive capacitor lead, and then to the input (left-hand) terminal of the voltage regulator.

❏ From the negative (-) DC rectifier terminal to the negative capacitor lead, then to the center terminal of the voltage regulator, and finally to one solder lug on the light socket.

❏ From the output (right-hand) terminal of the voltage regulator to the other solder lug on the light socket.

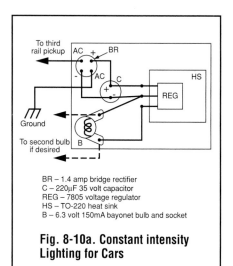

BR – 1.4 amp bridge rectifier
C – 220µF 35 volt capacitor
REG – 7805 voltage regulator
HS – TO-220 heat sink
B – 6.3 volt 150mA bayonet bulb and socket

Fig. 8-10a. Constant intensity Lighting for Cars

Fig. 8-10b. Constant-Intensity Lighting Circuit Mounted, but Not Wired

COMBINED DIRECTIONAL AND NONDIRECTIONAL LIGHTING

You can modify the circuit shown in fig. 8-3 to provide directional lighting for headlights and nondirectional lighting for number boards. Simply add another assembly of two 1-amp diodes to power the number board bulbs. See fig. 8-11. These diodes ensure that current always flows through the bulbs at 1.2 volts. Connect the number board bulbs in parallel, and mount them on

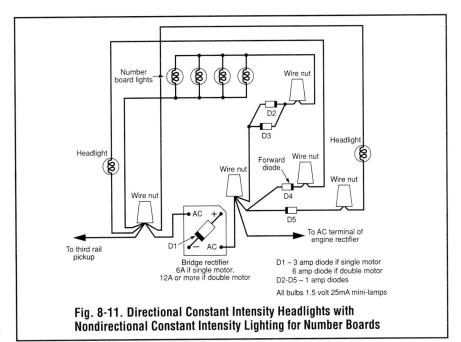

D1 – 3 amp diode if single motor
6 amp diode if double motor
D2-D5 – 1 amp diodes

All bulbs 1.5 volt 25mA mini-lamps

Fig. 8-11. Directional Constant Intensity Headlights with Nondirectional Constant Intensity Lighting for Number Boards

Powered Engine

D1 – 3 amp diode if single motor
6 amp diode if double motor
D2-D4 – 1 amp diodes

All bulbs 1.5 volt 25mA mini-lamps

Dummy Engine

D – 1 amp diode
C – 220µF 35 volt capacitor
REG – 7805 (5 volt) voltage regulator
HS – TO-220 heat sink
B – 6 volt 25mA mini-lamp

BR – 1.4 amp100 PIV bridge rectifier
C – 220µF 35 volt capacitor
REG – 7805 voltage regulator
HS – TO-220 heat sink
B1, B2 – 6 volt 25mA mini-lamps

Fig. 8-12. Complete Lighting System: AA Diesels with DC Polarity Reverse

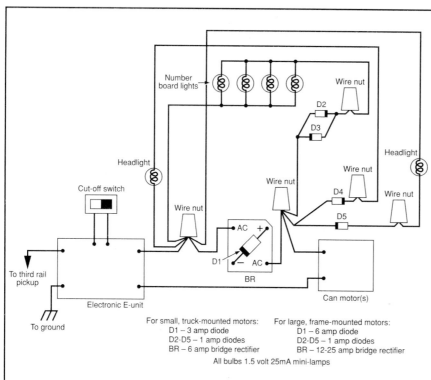

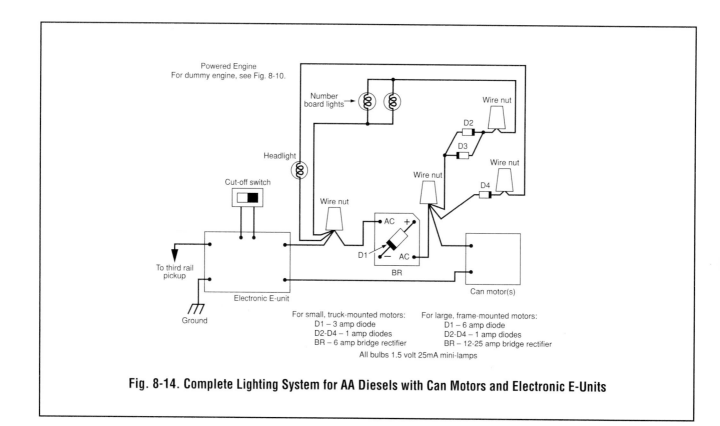

For small, truck-mounted motors:
D1 – 3 amp diode
D2-D5 – 1 amp diodes
BR – 6 amp bridge rectifier

For large, frame-mounted motors:
D1 – 6 amp diode
D2-D5 – 1 amp diodes
BR – 12-25 amp bridge rectifier

All bulbs 1.5 volt 25mA mini-lamps

Fig. 8-13. Combined Directional and Nondirectional Constant Intensity Lighting for Engines with Can Motors and Electronic E-Units

brackets like the headlight bulbs.

You can equip AA diesels with combined directional and nondirectional lighting. Wire the powered engine according to fig. 8-12. Use 6-volt, 25-milliamp mini lamps (272-1140) in the dummy engine, one for the headlight and two for the number boards. The left-hand circuit in fig. 8-12 powers the headlight, while the right-hand circuit powers the number boards.

Engines powered by can motors and electronic E-units can also use these lighting circuits. Follow figs. 8-13 or 8-14, whichever is applicable. Some engines already have directional diodes attached to their motor leads, and you may be able to use one in the circuit. Be aware that dummy engines operated on AC can have constant intensity but not directional lighting. Use the circuit in fig. 8-10.

For small, truck-mounted motors:
D1 – 3 amp diode
D2-D4 – 1 amp diodes
BR – 6 amp bridge rectifier

For large, frame-mounted motors:
D1 – 6 amp diode
D2-D4 – 1 amp diodes
BR – 12-25 amp bridge rectifier

All bulbs 1.5 volt 25mA mini-lamps

Fig. 8-14. Complete Lighting System for AA Diesels with Can Motors and Electronic E-Units

Appendix A

Glossary

AC (alternating current). Current that changes its direction at regular intervals. In North America, alternating current changes its direction 120 times a second.

Alternation. A single pulse of alternating current. Two alternations, one positive and one negative, form one cycle of AC.

Anode. The positive pole of a polarized device.

Ampere. The standard unit of electrical current. Abbreviated A, but commonly called an "amp."

Armature. The rotating element in a DC or universal motor. Also the movable steel bar in a doorbell.

Axial lead capacitor. A capacitor with a single lead coming out of each end.

Base. The terminal of a transistor through which a weak control current is applied.

Back emf (back electromotive force). A momentary high voltage that appears across the terminals of a coil when the current is suddenly turned off. Unless controlled, back emf can damage parts not designed to withstand it.

Bridge rectifier. A solid-state device consisting of four diodes that converts the entire flow of an alternating current into direct current. Also called a full-wave rectifier.

Brushes. Small cylinders that carry current to the commutator in a motor. Together, the brushes and commutator act as a switch, alternating the connections to the armature coils.

Can motor. A permanent magnet DC motor housed in cylindrical case. Can motors have increasingly replaced universal motors in tinplate locomotives.

Capacitor. A two-terminal electronic device that acts as a temporary storage tank for electrons.

Capacitor discharge (CD) unit. A circuit that charges and then discharges a large capacitor in order to generate a brief burst of heavy current. Capacitor discharge units can be used to power tinplate switches.

Cathode. The negative pole of a polarized device.

Collector. One of two terminals that carry the working current of a transistor. In an NPN transistor, the working current flows from the collector to the emitter. In a PNP transistor the flow of current is reversed. *See also* **Emitter.**

Commutator. A segmented bronze disk or ring that transmits electricity to the armature coils of a universal or DC motor.

Constant-intensity lighting. A lighting system whose brightness is not affected by changes in track voltage.

Control current. A small current flowing through the base of a transistor, which controls a heavier current flowing through its collector and emitter. *See also* **Working current.**

DC (direct current). Current that flows in one direction only.

Diode. A two-terminal device that allows current to flow in one direction only. *See also* **Half-wave rectifier.**

Directional lighting. A lighting circuit that illuminates only the forward headlight of a moving locomotive.

DPDT (double pole, double throw) switch. A switch with six terminals in two rows of three. When thrown, it connects each center terminal to either of two end terminals in the same row. A DPDT switch may be considered two parallel SPDT switches in the same housing, controlled by the same lever.

Double-wound field. A field coil consisting of two coils of wire wound in opposite directions. The direction of motor rotation depends on which coil is placed in the circuit. Motors with double-wound fields use two-position E-units.

Electrolytic capacitor. A type of polarized capacitor that uses an internal chemical solution or paste in its operation.

Electromagnet. A coil of insulated wire wound on an iron or steel core that produces a magnetic field when current is passed through it.

Emf. Abbreviation for *electromotive force. See* **Voltage.**

Emi. Abbreviation for *electromagnetic interference.* Unwanted radio emissions that can interfere with the operation of electronic circuits. Also called "noise," or "radio frequency interference (rfi)".

Emitter. One of two terminals that carry the working current of a transistor. In an NPN transistor, current flows from the collector to the emitter. In a PNP transistor, current flows in the opposite direction. *See also* **Collector.**

E-10. Generic term for a screw-base bulb or socket the same size as the type Lionel used until about 1950.

E-unit. Lionel's name for the reversing relay installed in its locomotives. Also an electronic reversing circuit used in conjunction with can motors.

Farad. The standard unit of capacitance, that is, of the ability of a capacitor to store an electric charge. Abbreviated F. *See also* **Microfarad.**

Field. *See* **Field coil.**

Field coil. The stationary electromagnet in a universal or DC motor.

Filter capacitor. A large capacitor used to convert the pulsating direct current that emerges from a rectifier into a relatively smooth flow.

Gate. The terminal of a triac through which a current is applied to turn the device on.

Ground. A common return path for electricity. In tinplate applications, the metal frames and wheels of locomotives and cars, together with the running rails of the track, serve as the ground. Also used as a verb, meaning "to connect to a ground."

Half-wave rectifier. A single diode used as a rectifier. Its name comes from the fact that it passes only half of the AC current wave.

Heatsink. A device used to carry away unwanted heat.

Hertz (abbreviated Hz). Cycles per second.

Interrupter. The armature and contact assembly in a doorbell.

K. Abbreviation for *kilohm.* One thousand ohms.

Lead. A wire protruding from an electronic device, providing a connection to it.

LED. Abbreviation for *light-emitting diode.* A two-terminal solid-state device that generates a colored light when a small direct current is passed through it.

Lug. *See* **Solder lug.**

Main terminals (1 and 2). The two terminals of a triac through which a heavy current flows after a momentary pulse is applied at the gate. Also called "anode 1" and "anode 2."

Microfarad. One millionth of a farad. Abbreviated μF.

Milliampere. One thousandth of an ampere. Abbreviated mA, but often called a "milliamp."

Millisecond. One thousandth of a second.

Momentary switch. A switch that is thrown only for the time that its handle or button is held down.

Nondirectional lighting. A circuit that illuminates engine headlights, regardless of the direction in which the engine moves.

Normally closed. A term applied to a relay or switch whose contacts are closed until the switch is thrown or the relay is energized.

Normally open. A term applied to a relay or switch whose contacts are open until the switch is thrown or the relay is energized.

Observing polarity. Connecting a polarized device properly.

Ohm. The standard unit of resistance to the flow of electrical current. Abbreviated Ω.

Parallel circuit. A circuit whose components are connected like the rungs of a ladder, "in parallel," sharing the same positive and negative terminals.

Peak inverse voltage (PIV). The highest voltage that a diode can withstand from a current flowing in what is normally its non-conducting direction.

Phase control. A technique for controlling AC power by varying the point during each alternation that the current is switched on.

Picofarad. One millionth of a microfarad. Abbreviated pF.

Pinout. A diagram of the pins in a relay or integrated circuit.

PIV. *See* **Peak inverse voltage.**

Polarized. Having a positive and a negative pole. Diodes and electrolytic capacitors are polarized devices.

Pot. *See* **Potentiometer,**

Potentiometer. A variable resistor, whose resistance is set by moving an internal wiper, either with a screwdriver or by turning a knob. Commonly called a "pot."

Power diode. *See* **Rectifier diode.**

Radial lead capacitor. A capacitor with both leads coming out of the same end

RC circuit. Abbreviation for *resistance capacitance circuit.* An arrangement of one or more resistors and capacitors used to time an electrical output.

Rectifier. A device that converts alternating current to direct current.

Rectifier diode. A diode rated at 1 or more amps, whether or not it is in fact used as a rectifier. Also called a power diode.

Relay. A switch operated by an internal electromagnet

Resistor. A device designed to restrict the flow of current. The resistance of a resistor is measured in ohms, and its ability to dissipate heat, in watts.

Rosin. A substance in some solders designed to clean joints and enable the solder to flow and adhere better.

Series circuit. A circuit whose components are connected end to end, "in series," like beads on a necklace.

Solenoid. A hollow electromagnet that uses a movable steel plunger as its core.

SPDT (single pole, double throw) switch. A three-terminal switch that, when thrown, connects its center terminal to either of two end terminals.

SPST (single pole, single throw) switch. A simple off-on switch.

Solder lug. A small metal tab to which a wire can be soldered. Some solder lugs are built into other devices, while others are available separately, often with holes for attaching them to terminal screws or binding posts. Solder lugs make electrical connections more reliable.

Third-rail pickup. The shoe or roller which carries current from the third rail of tinplate track to a motor in an engine or to a light or other device in a car. Also the wire connected to such a shoe or roller.

Three-position E-unit. A reversing relay with a neutral as well as a forward and a reverse position. It reverses the direction of motor rotation by alternating the connections to the brushes. Lionel installed three-position E-Units in locomotives whose field coils had only a single winding.

Transistor. A three-terminal solid-state device that allows a small current to control a much larger current.

Triac. A three-terminal solid-state device used to switch alternating current.

Trigger switch. A solid-state device used to turn a triac on. A bilateral trigger switch turns the triac on at some point during each alternation of AC.

Trimmer pot. A small potentiometer designed for occasional adjustment with a screwdriver.

Two-position E-unit. A reversing relay with only a forward and a reverse position. Lionel installed two-position E-units in locomotives whose motors had double-wound fields.

Universal motor. A motor that can operate on either alternating current or direct current.

Volt. The standard unit of electrical pressure. Abbreviated V.

Voltage. Electrical pressure. Also called electromotive force (emf).

Watt. The standard unit of electrical power. Wattage is computed by multiplying amperes and volts. Since unused power is released as heat, wattage ratings of components are critical in circuit construction. Abbreviated W.

Working current. The heavy current controlled by a transistor. The working current flows through the collector and emitter of the device. *See also* **Control current.**

Appendix B

Short List of Mail-Order Suppliers

Digi-Key Corporation
701 Brooks Ave. S.
P. O. Box 677
Thief River Falls, MN 56701-0677
Phone orders and catalogs: (800) 344-4539
Free bimonthly catalog; $5 handling charge for orders under $25. No ship-
ping and handling charge for orders over $25 when paid by check.

Hosfelt Electronics
2700 Sunset Blvd.
Steubenville, OH 43952-1158
Phone orders and catalogs: (800) 524-5414
Free catalog issued every six months; shipping and handling charge

Jameco Electronic Components/Computer Products
1355 Shoreway Rd.
Belmont, CA 94002-4100
Phone orders and catalogs: (800) 831-4242
Free catalog; shipping charge. Jameco also sells parts through a retail distri-
bution network. See catalog for details.

Mouser Electronics
958 N. Main St.
Mansfield, TX 76063-4827
Phone orders and catalogs: (800) 346-6873
Free catalog issued quarterly; shipping charge.

For a more complete list of suppliers, see Peter J. Thorne, *Model Railroad
Electronics: Basic Concepts to Advanced Projects.*

Appendix C

List of of References

Barker, Thomas B. 1983. *Greenberg's American Flyer S Gauge Operating and Repair Manual, 1945–1965, 2nd ed.* Greenberg Publishing Company, Sykesville, Md.

Fiehmann, Don, with Frank Geraci and Sandy Fiehmann. 1988. *Basic Electricity and Electronics for Model Railroaders.* Kalmbach Books, Waukesha, Wis. (out of print)

Greenberg's Repair & Operating Manual For Lionel Trains, 1945–1969. Greenberg Publishing Co., Sykesville, Md.

Hubbard, John G. 1981. *Greenberg's Repair and Operating Manual: Prewar Lionel Trains.* Greenberg Publishing Company, Sykesville, Md.

Kouba, John H. 1992. 1992. *Greenberg's Model Railroading with Lionel Trains, Volume II: An Advanced Layout.* Greenberg Publishing Company, Sykesville, Md.

LaVoie, Roland E. 1989. *Greenberg's Model Railroading with Lionel Trains.* Greenberg Publishing Company, Sykesville, Md.

Lionel Corporation, Editorial Staff. 1990. *Model Railroading, 5th ed.* Greenberg Publishing Company, Sykesville, Md. (out of print)

Mallery, Paul. 1971. *Electrical Handbook for Model Railroads, Vol. 1.* Carstens Publications, Newton, N.J.

Mallery, Paul. 1983. *Electrical Handbook for Model Railroads, Vol. 2.* Carstens Publications, Newton, N.J.

Mims, Forrest M., III. 1980. *Engineer's Mini-Notebook: Schematic Symbols, Device Packages, Design and Testing.* Radio Shack, Fort Worth, Texas.

Plummer, Ray H. 1990. "Big power for a small price." In *Classic Toy Trains*, vol. 3, no. 5 (October 1990), 75–77.

Plummer, Ray H. 1993. "Snap those 'starter set' switches: Constant fixed voltage for O-27 switches." In *Classic Toy Trains*, vol. 6, no. 3 (May 1993), 104–105.

Riddle, Peter H. 1991. *Greenberg's Wiring Your Lionel Layout, Vol. I: A Primer for Lionel Enthusiasts.* Greenberg Publishing Company, Sykesville, Md.

Riddle, Peter H. 1993. *Greenberg's Wiring Your Lionel Layout, Vol. II: Intermediate Techniques.* Kalmbach Books, Waukesha, Wis.

Riddle, Peter H. 1996. *Greenberg's Wiring Your Lionel Layout, Vol. III: Advanced Technologies Made Easy.* Kalmbach Publishing Co., Waukesha, Wis.

Riddle, Peter H. 1994. *Tips and Tricks for Toy Train Operators.* Kalmbach Publishing Co., Waukesha, Wis.

Smith, Phillip K., and Stan Shantar. 1982. *Greenberg's Enjoying Lionel-Fundimensions Trains.* Greenberg Publishing Company, Sykesville, Md. (out of print)

Thorne, Peter J. 1974. *Practical Electronic Projects for Model Railroaders.* Kalmbach Books, Milwaukee, Wis. (out of print)

Thorne, Peter J. 1982. *34 New Electronic Projects for Model Railroaders.* Kalmbach Books, Milwaukee, Wis. (out of print)

Thorne, Peter J. 1988. *Easy-to-Build Electronic Projects for Model Railroaders.* Kalmbach Books, Waukesha, Wis. (out of print)

Thorne, Peter J. 1994. *Model Railroad Electronics: Basic Concepts to Advanced Projects.* Kalmbach Books, Waukesha, Wis.

Weatherford, Jim. 1989. *Lionel Repair: Your Step-by-Step Maintenance Guide, Vols. 2 and 3.* Pasadena, Calif.: Act Video (videotapes).

Weaver, Carl. 1992. *Greenberg's Model Railroading with Märklin HO.* Greenberg Publishing Company, Sykesville, Md.

Note: We have indicated Kalmbach and Greenberg titles which are known to be out of print at press time. Some of these titles may still be available at hobby stores or from used-book dealers at swap meets or train shows.

Index